HONG KONG

A View of a Remarkable City

LEE H. VAN DAM

HONG KONG – A View of a Remarkable City

Art by Suzanne Nikolaisen
Book design by Robyne Gallacher
Copyright © 2020 by Lee H. Van Dam

Published in the United States by
LHVD Books
Sandy, Utah
www.lhvdbooks.com

ISBN: 978-0-9903610-4-6

Library of Congress Control Number 2020903742

Also by the author –

Cruising – A View Through the Porthole
Golfing – A View Through the Golf Hole

Contents

Experiencing Hong Kong

Hong Kong is a remarkable city – certainly one of the most interesting places in the world! I am often asked by friends who are planning to visit Hong Kong for the first time for advice on how best to see and experience this amazing place. Since traveling tastes are very individual things, it is not easy to give advice that suits everyone. Some people are sightseers, some want to spend time in museums, and some want to experience more of the people and the culture. Me? I am a bit of a combination of these. **I want to see all of the interesting sights, but I also want to be able to gain an understanding of the people and their way of life.** So, with that in mind, here are a few of my thoughts about how I would spend my time if I were visiting Hong Kong for the first time.

When is a good time to go? Hong Kong's climate is an important consideration in planning your trip. With a cooler winter and a very hot and humid summer, **fall and spring are the better times to travel there.** Ideal months are October, November, March, and April, unless you want to be there for some of the big Chinese festivals such as Chinese New Year (in late January or early February) or the Dragon Boat Festival (in May or June).

Where should we stay? Being in a hotel that has a wonderful view of the harbor would be my first choice. However, hotels like that will be on the expensive end of the scale since Hong Kong is one of the costliest cities in the world. But Hong Kong has hundreds of hotel and lodging choices offering thousands of hotel rooms ranging from extremely expensive to very cheap, so finding one to your liking that fits your budget shouldn't be a problem. Here are some possible choices:

- **Very Expensive**
  - o **Peninsula Hotel** – This would be my first choice in Hong Kong if money were no object. It is a stylish cultural icon that has a prime location at the tip of the Kowloon Peninsula. **The Peninsula oozes old-world charm and ambiance.** If you want to be pampered and get a feel for Hong Kong as it was in colonial times, this is the place. (A similar grand old hotel is the Mandarin Hotel on the island.)
  - o **Ritz-Carlton** – Located on the 102nd through 118th floors of the International Commerce Centre in Kowloon, this is **the highest hotel in the world** located in a skyscraper. The views in every direction are terrific and the amenities and restaurants are superb.
  - o **Four Seasons** – On Hong Kong island, this wonderful hotel is housed in the International Finance Centre in the Central District. It has excellent views of the harbor and Kowloon and its Lung King Heen Restaurant was **the world's first Chinese restaurant to be awarded three Michelin stars.**

- **Expensive**
  - o **Island Shangri-La** – With a prime island location and excellent views, this is a wonderful hotel. It is famous for two things: (1) **a 16-story painted silk mural called** *Great Motherland of China,* which is the largest such piece of artwork in the world; and (2) **a 140-year-old banyan tree in the hotel's atrium.** Some HK$24 million (US$3.1 million) was spent to preserve the tree while the hotel was being built.
  - o **InterContinental Hong Kong** – With a superb waterfront location on the Kowloon side, this hotel is close to Nathan Road, the Avenue of the Stars, the Star Ferry, and many upscale shops and restaurants.
  - o **Grand Hyatt Hong Kong** – Connected to the Convention and Exhibition Centre on the island, this hotel has a wonderful vista of the harbor and is considered to be an

excellent value for the money. It is close to some of the old markets and quaint shopping streets on the island.

- **Moderate**
  - **YMCA on Salisbury Road** – This surprisingly upscale hotel is located directly adjacent to the Peninsula Hotel in Kowloon and has essentially the same view and location as the Peninsula, but at a fraction of the Peninsula's price. **This is where Holly and I stayed on our last visit to Hong Kong and we loved it. Book early and ask for a harbor view room on a high floor.** That type of room is worth the little bit of extra cost. The hotel has a swimming pool, exercise room, and restaurant, and is convenient to everything. It is newly remodeled and very comfortable.
  - **Novotel Century Hong Kong** – This has clean, comfortable rooms and is in a good location on the island. It has no views, but it is close to restaurants, shopping, and transportation.

- o **Holiday Inn Golden Mile** – Located directly on Nathan Road in Kowloon, this popular hotel is right in the middle of the busy tourist stretch of Tsim Sha Tsui – and it is convenient to many tailors if you're looking for a suit and some shirts.

- **Inexpensive** (but in Hong Kong even inexpensive things can cost quite a bit)
  - o **Metropark Hotel** – Located on Waterloo Road in Kowloon, this hotel provides a clean and comfortable place to stay at a good value. It is located within easy walking distance of the Ladies Street area.
  - o **Butterfly on Victoria Hotel** – Located near Victoria Park in Causeway Bay on the island, this boutique hotel provides a pleasant place to stay. Although not near the typical tourist areas, it is close to an MTR stop, so getting around is easy. The smaller rooms in this hotel are relatively quiet (it's hard in Hong Kong to ever find true quiet) and they are nicely furnished.
  - o **Caritas Bianchi Lodge** – In Yau Ma Tei on the Kowloon side, this is a clean and friendly hostel offering rooms with private baths. The Jade Market, Temple Street Night Market, and Mong Kong Computer Centre are within easy walking distance. This place fills up fast, so book early.

How long should we stay? It is hard to discover Hong Kong in a meaningful way in just a day or two, so I recommend you spend **at least three full days** experiencing Hong Kong's sights, sounds, tastes, and people. This can be done on your own at your own pace, which is how I prefer to see things, or you can sign up for any number of commercial tours to do it. A suggested itinerary for each day would be:

- **Day 1 (Suit, Chop, and Hong Kong Island)**
  - o **Buy a Suit** – Get fitted for a suit at one of Hong Kong's many tailor shops. By doing this on the first day, you'll leave time for an additional fitting or two so that your suit will be just the way you want it. You may want to study up a bit on suits before your trip. At home, look at suits in clothing stores and study men's fashion magazines so you'll have a good idea of what kinds of fabrics, colors,

and styles are your favorites. If you'd like a suggestion for a tailor, the one I go to is Ash Samtani Clothing at 92-94 Nathan Road, Burlington Arcade, in Tsim Sha Tsui on the Kowloon side. I bought my first suit there in April of 1966 and have been using them since. And you are welcome to mention to Ash, Luke, and Amar Samtani that I recommended them to you.

o **Order a Chop** – Have a Chinese person who speaks good English give you a Chinese name consisting of three Chinese characters. Then order a Chinese chop from one of the many small shops that make them. A chop is a traditional Chinese signature stamp with your Chinese name etched into it. Going there on your first day will give the shopkeeper time to have the chop carved and ready for you before you leave town.

o **Ride the Star Ferry** – This world-famous ferry has been going back and forth across Hong Kong's harbor since 1888. I love the Star Ferry and try to ride it each time I visit Hong Kong. And I especially enjoy riding it at night.

o **Go to the Peak** – Take the Peak Tram (it is actually a funicular) to the top of Victoria Peak and then go up the escalators in the Peak Tower to the viewing deck. If your time in Hong Kong permits, go to the Peak twice – once in the day and then again at night.

o **Visit Repulse Bay and Stanley Market** – Take the #6 or #260 bus from Central to Stanley Market. Try to sit on the top deck at the very front of the bus so you'll have the best view.

- **Day 2 (Kowloon and the New Territories)**
  o **Mong Kok Shopping Area – Shop in the Mong Kok area on the Kowloon side at Ladies Street, Sneakers Street, Flower Market Street, Bird Street, etc.** And if you like electronics, don't miss the Mong Kok Computer Centre at #8 Nelson Street. It is a congested, jam-packed, shoulder-to-shoulder mall where you'll find every conceivable kind of computer and electronic product. It's a little hard to spot. Enter on the ground floor and then go upstairs.
  o **Jade Market** – The Jade Market is a lot of fun to visit. The many shops in this congested market specialize in

offering an unbelievable variety of jade pieces in many shapes, colors, and price ranges. They also sell pearls and other jewelry.

o **Ten Thousand Buddhas Temple** – Located in Sha Tin in the New Territories, this is an interesting place to experience old Chinese culture and learn about Chinese beliefs.

o **A Symphony of Lights** – Held every evening at 8:00 p.m. at Victoria Harbour, this light and sound show can be seen from either side of the harbor, although I prefer viewing it from the Kowloon side.

o **Tsim Sha Tsui and Kowloon at Night** – Shop the many stores and markets along Nathan Road in Tsim Sha Tsui. Ride a double-decker bus headed north on Nathan Road to the area of the Temple Street Night Market. Sit on the top deck of the bus in the front seat!

- **Day 3 (Lantau Island and Farewell Dinner)**
  o **Big Buddha** – Take the MTR to Tung Chung on Lantau Island and then ride the Ngong Ping 360 cable car to the Big Buddha statue. Hike the 268 steps to the Big Buddha, eat a vegetarian lunch at the Po Lin Monastery, and stroll through the shops at Ngong Ping Village.
  o **Suit and Chop** – Pick up your suit and chop.
  o **Peking Duck Dinner** – Finish off your trip to Hong Kong with a Peking duck dinner at a fancy Chinese restaurant such as the Peking Garden Restaurant in Star House on the Kowloon side near the Star Ferry. (Note – You may need to make reservations and place your order in advance if you plan on having Peking duck.)

For those whose travel plans allow them to stay for a longer period of time in Hong Kong, or for those who are lucky enough to live in Hong Kong, please see my list of **101 Things to See and Do in Hong Kong (Appendix D).**

Chinese Term

Double Happiness

Seen prominently at Chinese weddings and elsewhere, the double happiness symbol is a beautiful Chinese artistic design made up of **two characters for the word joy placed side by side.** Its presence is believed to bring extra happiness and harmony.

The double happiness symbol (usually in bright red or gold) appears frequently at Hong Kong weddings on invitations, decorations, and favors – and often even in the fabric of the bride's dress and the material used to make the groom's clothing. It is also commonly displayed in homes, in businesses, and on many Chinese products.

Oh, Bring Back My Hong Kong to Me

After being under British rule for 156 years, Hong Kong was handed back to China on July 1, 1997 in a ceremony in Hong Kong attended by Britain's Prince Charles, Hong Kong's Governor Chris Patten, and the People's Republic of China's (PRC) President Jiang Zemin. Despite Britain's desire that the 99-year lease on the New Territories be renewed and extended, the Chinese government was not willing to do so. They wanted everything back – all of the areas the world had come to know as Hong Kong, which included:

- Hong Kong Island – ceded by the Chinese to the British in 1842
- Kowloon – acquired by the British from China in 1860
- The New Territories – leased from China in 1898 for 99 years

Thus, all of Hong Kong, which had existed for so long on borrowed soil and borrowed time, went back under Chinese rule.

Just before midnight on June 30, 1997 in the new wing of the Hong Kong Convention and Exhibition Centre located on the island, the British Union Jack and the flag of the British colony of Hong Kong were slowly lowered as a British military band played *God Save the Queen.* Then China's red flag with yellow stars and Hong Kong's newly created red flag with a white bauhinia flower on it were raised as a Chinese military band played *The March of the Volunteers,* China's national anthem.

A few minutes later, Prince Charles and Governor Chris Patten stepped on board the royal yacht Britannia and sailed out of Victoria Harbour, **ending Britain's rule of Hong Kong.**

As I ponder that scene, my mind's eye pictures **Her Majesty, Queen Elizabeth II** – 71 years of age at the time of the handover – in Buckingham Palace in London just before the clock strikes midnight in far off Hong Kong, wearing her crown, looking crestfallen as she sadly sings this song:

Oh, Bring Back My Hong Kong to Me
Sung to *My Bonnie Lies over the Ocean*
Words by Lee H. Van Dam

My Hong Kong lies over the ocean,
My Hong Kong lies over the sea.
My Hong Kong has gone back to China,
Oh, bring back my Hong Kong to me.

Bring back, bring back,
Oh, bring back my Hong Kong to me, to me.
Bring back, bring back,
Oh, bring back my Hong Kong to me.

We made lots of money in Hong Kong,
With help of a really long lease.
The people became very wealthy,
So why does our reign have to cease?

Refrain

I loved going shopping in Stanley,
The things there were often so cheap.
I always have loved a good bargain,
But now I just sit back and weep.

Refrain

My Hong Kong was full of good eating,
Please give me another dim sum.
I've always enjoyed Chinese tasties,
Oh, Hong Kong was really our plum.

Refrain

The sun never set on my empire,
My smile has now turned to a frown.
On the beautiful place that is Hong Kong,
My sun has now finally gone down.

Refrain

My Hong Kong lies over the ocean,

My Hong Kong lies over the sea.
My Hong Kong has gone back to China,
Oh, bring back my Hong Kong to me.

Refrain

It has now been over 20 years since Hong Kong was returned to China. **As part of the handover transaction, China agreed to keep most things essentially the same for a period of 50 years.** Specifically, China said that Hong Kong would enjoy a high degree of autonomy, except in foreign affairs and defense, and that China's socialist system would not be imposed on Hong Kong. **They designated Hong Kong as a Special Administrative Region (SAR) of China and said that it would keep its own capitalist system, police, and judiciary.** The head of the SAR would be a Chinese resident of Hong Kong in place of a governor appointed by the British. This person would be called the chief executive.

With those promises in mind, let's take a look at some things that have stayed the same and some things that have changed.

What are some of the things that have stayed the same?

- **Street and Location Names** – Despite the handover to the Chinese, the many British-influenced street and location names in Hong Kong have not been changed. There still is Prince Edward Road (named after Prince Edward VIII after he visited Hong Kong in 1922), Victoria Peak and Victoria Harbour (Victoria was the queen of the United Kingdom from 1837 to 1901), Admiralty (the area of the island where the British navy's dockyard was located), and Cornwall Street (Cornwall is a county in the UK). **The Chinese government has made no attempt to change or rename these, or other, British-themed places in Hong Kong.**
- **The Press – Hong Kong has a reputation for having one of the largest and most diverse press industries in the world.** A free and open press is still one of Hong Kong's trademarks, although a degree of censorship by the Chinese government has been creeping in. Dozens of Chinese and English language newspapers and periodicals are published that continue to represent a great variety of opinions and political views. Despite the growing influence of Beijing, pro-democracy and pro-capitalist publications are still allowed.

- **Currency** – The currency in mainland China is the yuan. **The currency in Hong Kong is the Hong Kong dollar,** which is pegged to the U.S. dollar. There has been no movement by the mainland government to make the yuan the currency of Hong Kong.

- **Customs and Immigration Regulations** – The border with mainland China, **now known as the boundary,** continues to be patrolled as before with the two entities (Hong Kong and the PRC) having separate customs and immigration controls.

- **Law System** – Hong Kong remains **a common-law jurisdiction** with a separate legal system from mainland China.

- **Wigs** – Wigs? Why would I bring up wigs here? Influenced by judicial traditions in Great Britain, **judges and barristers in Hong Kong have long worn white curled horsehair wigs while serving in the highest courts.** Such an obvious British thing was thought to be one of the first traditions that would be discarded after the handover. But more than 20 years on, those beloved wigs are still there and the Chinese in the mainland haven't batted an eye about them.

- **Official Languages** – **Hong Kong's two official languages remain Chinese and English** and street names and public documents continue to be written in both Chinese and English. Cantonese is still the primary spoken language. Although Mandarin is not the dominant spoken language of Hong Kong (like it is in mainland China), Mandarin is becoming much more common and is a basic language course now taught in Hong Kong schools.

- **Religious Freedom** – Hong Kong, which has always had a great diversity of religious beliefs and practices, **continues to have religious freedom,** much the same as it did before the handover.

- **Driving on the Left Side** – Even though vehicles are driven on the right side of the road in mainland China, in Hong Kong they are still driven the British way – **on the left side.**

- **Travel to China** – Hong Kong citizens are still required to obtain a permit in order to visit China. The permit is now called a **Mainland Travel Permit.**

- **Stock Exchange** – Hong Kong still has its own **stock exchange.** Its index is called the Hang Seng Index.

What are some of the things that have changed?

- **Holidays** – The holidays of the Queen's Birthday and Liberation Day have been replaced by **Hong Kong SAR Establishment Day** (July 1) and **PRC National Day** (October 1).

- **Queen Elizabeth's Image and the Crown** – Queen Elizabeth II's head no longer appears on Hong Kong coins and currency and her portrait has been removed from public offices. **Coins now have the bauhinia flower on them.** The crown has been replaced by a bauhinia flower on the crest of the Hong Kong police force.

- **Stamps** – Hong Kong postage stamps now have the words **"Hong Kong, China"** written on them.

- **The Military** – Replacing British overseas forces, the defense of Hong Kong is now the responsibility of China's **People's Liberation Army,** which has a garrison in Hong Kong.

- **Demonstrations** – As has been evident in the news, Hong Kong's residents have staged a number of protests and demonstrations in the past few years. Although the people of Hong Kong still have the right to gather and demonstrate (under certain conditions), **the new government is not as lenient and patient with political demonstrators as before.** Hong Kong continues to have more political freedoms than mainland China, but free speech in Hong Kong is not quite as free as it used to be.

- **New Airport** – A huge new airport was completed in 1998, replacing the old Kai Tak airport in Kowloon. **The new airport was built largely on reclaimed land situated just off of Lantau Island.**

- **International Sporting Events** – At the Olympics and other international sporting events, **Hong Kong is now known as Hong Kong, China.** The athletes compete under the Hong Kong SAR flag instead of the British flag of Hong Kong. **Gold medalists, if any, are now honored with the Chinese national anthem.**

- **Visas for British Citizens** – Other than those with a right of abode, **visas are now required for British citizens to work in Hong Kong.**

- **The Feel and Culture of Hong Kong** – The city's feel and culture are changing. As more and more mainland Chinese people move to Hong Kong, and as their influence in the city grows, **the customs, foods, stores, and way of life are changing.** This was to be expected, of course, but many people who were born in Hong Kong or who have resided in the city for many years are somewhat troubled by these changes and would prefer to have things remain as they were.

On July 1, 1997, Hong Kong ceased being a British Crown Colony. Since then, it has been a Special Administrative Region (SAR) of China, being operated under a policy that allows Hong Kong to remain capitalist while mainland China is socialist. The Chinese government calls this a **"one country, two systems"** form of government.

(Note – **Perhaps you'll recall that even James Bond got involved in the handover.** In the book *Zero Minus Ten*, Bond is dispatched to Hong Kong in 1997 to help avert a potential international crisis related to the handover. He receives the assignment just 10 days before the event, hence the name of the book, *Zero Minus Ten*. On page 40 of the book, we learn something new and interesting about Agent 007. **He speaks Cantonese.** While giving him the assignment, M, his supervisor, asks "How's your Chinese?" James Bond answers, **"I speak Cantonese pretty well, ma'am, but I'm not so fluent in Mandarin."** The book is an interesting fictional read about events leading up to the July 1, 1997 handover to China.)

Chinese Term

Golden Phoenix Talons

"If you've ever eaten chicken feet, then you know the first sensation to greet you is the velvety smooth skin, so delicate it peels easily off of the diminutive bones. Following the tantalizing texture is the perky sweetness of the dish that will make your taste buds jump for joy. Finally, and unexpectedly, you'll be pleased by how succulent the tendons and ligaments are." – Eddie Lin, exotic food critic

In the Cantonese culture, it is common to use the word phoenix to mean chicken. **Golden Phoenix Talons, a dish in many Hong Kong dim sum restaurants, is a fancy name for chicken feet.** Chinese people believe that eating Golden Phoenix Talons improves a person's skin and bones. They especially think that women who are looking for better skin should eat chicken feet.

Chicken feet are hugely popular across China to the point that they simply can't get enough of them. China has over 8 billion chickens in their country (i.e. over 16 billion chicken feet), but that doesn't begin to keep up with the demand. **So, China imports lots of chicken feet.** Just the U.S. alone shipped more than 500,000 tons of chicken feet to them during a recent year. And China loves U.S. chicken feet because U.S. chickens are bred to be plump and large birds full of meat – **and plump and large birds full of meat have extra big and sturdy feet to hold them up.** Those are just the kind of feet the Chinese prefer.

Although just plain chicken feet can be ordered, it is the sauces they are simmered in that are a big part of their appeal. Popular sauces for chicken feet include fermented black bean sauce, minced ginger and anise sauce, and oyster sauce with brown sugar and garlic. Eddie Lin said one more interesting thing about eating Golden Phoenix Talons. He wrote, **"Eating chicken feet is like learning to tango with your tongue; only here a chicken foot is your dance partner."** Now isn't that an intriguing thought?

Hong Kong "Ests"

Each of the books I have written has included a chapter about **"ests."** In the cruise book, we discussed the **"ests"** of cruise ships (Chapter #12), in the golf book we reviewed the **"ests"** of golf courses (Chapter #4), so in this book I thought we'd talk about **Hong Kong's "ests."**

Hong Kong is a remarkable place. Although not very large, as of the date of this book **it has the distinction of being first in the world in a number of interesting categories, such as:**

1. **Highest IQ in the World** – The intelligence quotient (IQ) of the world's countries has been a topic of research by scholars over the years. Studies have indicated that **the highest average IQ of any country is Hong Kong** (Hong Kong is considered to be a country in the studies). **At an average estimated IQ of 107,** Hong Kong claims the top spot in the world, ahead of #2 South Korea and #3 Japan. And what about the U.S.? At an average IQ of 98, it ranks 19th in the world. And which state in the U.S. do you think has the highest average IQ? If you said Massachusetts, you'd be correct. That state's average IQ is estimated at 104.

2. **Most Rolls-Royces Per Capita** – Hong Kong holds the distinction of having **the most Rolls-Royce automobiles per capita of any place on the planet.** A good spot to see a number of them all at once is at the front entrance of the

Peninsula Hotel located at the tip of the Kowloon Peninsula. **The hotel has a fleet of 14 Rolls-Royce Phantom courtesy cars painted a special color called Peninsula green.** When the Peninsula purchased those luxury automobiles, **it was the largest single order ever placed with Rolls-Royce.**

3. **Largest Outdoor Bronze Seated Buddha – The Tian Tan Buddha (commonly referred to as the Big Buddha) on Lantau Island is the largest outdoor bronze seated Buddha in the world.** It is not the largest Buddha – it is the largest one that is outdoors, and bronze, and seated. Seated Buddhas are especially noteworthy because when Buddha

was attaining enlightenment over 2,500 years ago, **he was in a seated position under a Bodhi tree during the process,** so this is a favorite way to depict him. Another good display of Buddhas in Hong Kong is the **Ten Thousand Buddhas Monastery** in Sha Tin in the New Territories. (But be forewarned about getting to these two attractions. A climb of **268 steps** is required to go to the Big Buddha and a climb of **431 steps** is necessary to reach the 10,000 Buddhas – but both climbs are well worth the effort, in my opinion.)

4. **Most Skyscrapers – Hong Kong is in first place in the world by a large margin for its number of skyscrapers.** With a total of **355 skyscrapers,** it has 26% more than New York City, which is in second place, and 31% more than Shenzhen, which ranks third in the world. Many of Hong Kong's skyscrapers are wonderful examples of beautiful architectural design and innovation. I especially like the **Bank of China Tower** (often referred to as "The Chopsticks"), the **Lippo Centre** (nicknamed "The Koala Building"), and the 75-story **Highcliff** residential tower near the Happy Valley Race Course.

5. **Most Billionaires Per Capita –** By a wide margin, **Hong Kong has the most billionaires (that's billionaires with a "b") per capita of any place in the world.** With **67 of them** out of a population of only 7.5 million (one for every 112,000 people), Hong Kong surpasses all other countries, including the U.S., which has 585 billionaires out of a population of 330 million (one for every 564,000 people).

6. **Most Expensive Luxury Real Estate – At a staggering US$11,000 per square foot average, Hong Kong's luxury residential real estate is the most expensive in the world.** Attracting business moguls and investors from many countries, Hong Kong's luxury real estate market has skyrocketed, making it the most expensive anywhere. According to Forbes, the average footage of a billionaire's property on Hong Kong Island is 5,200 square feet, making the average price for a luxury home of that size **more than US$57 million.**

7. **Most Difficult Major Language to Learn –** Cantonese, the primary language of Hong Kong, is considered by many language experts to be **the most difficult major language to learn for a person whose native tongue is English.** This is

due to a variety of factors including its **seven tones,** its **complicated writing system,** and the fact that **Cantonese shares very little vocabulary with other languages.** In a ranking of language difficulty by the Defense Language Institute, **Cantonese is at the top,** followed by Mandarin (which has four tones), Arabic, Korean, and Japanese. One way of assessing the difficulty level of a language is by measuring how many hours of instruction are required to gain general speaking proficiency. And how many hours is that? **According to the Institute, at least 1,320 hours of dedicated study are required to learn Cantonese.** That's more than 165 eight-hour days of study.

8. **Busiest District – The Mong Kok area in Kowloon has been recognized by *Guinness World Records* as the busiest and most densely populated district in the world with a population of over 340,000 people per square mile** – and this figure doesn't include the many thousands of tourists who flock there daily. Mong Kok, which translates as **"busy corner"** in Cantonese, is a noisy, lively, and fascinating place to shop for bargains in clothing, purses, electronics, toys, luggage, phones, and athletic shoes.

9. **Cheapest Michelin Star Restaurant – The Tim Ho Wan dim sum restaurant** has the distinction of being **the world's cheapest Michelin star restaurant.** Now with several locations, the first one was a small 20-seat hole-in-the-wall in Mong Kok where dim sum was available for less than US$5.

10. **World's Highest Hotel – The Ritz-Carlton Hong Kong Hotel, located on the Kowloon side, is the highest hotel in the world located in a skyscraper.** The hotel's 312 rooms occupy the top 17 floors (floors 102-118) of the International Commerce Centre. Showcasing spectacular views, exquisite restaurants, and extensive amenities, **it is truly a marvelous hotel.** And if you go there, make sure to notice the stunning artwork on the ceiling of the hotel's lobby. Named *Horses Galloping Across the Sky,* these ink and brush masterpieces were painted by the world-renowned Chinese artist **Yaunming He.** It is interesting to note that **the manes and tails of each of the horses were painted with one single stroke of the artist's brush.**

And why stop at just ten **"ests"**? Hong Kong also has:

- The world's largest permanent light and sound show (*A Symphony of Lights* **presented nightly over Victoria Harbour).**
- The largest painted silk mural in the world **(a magnificent 16-story-high silk painting titled *Great Motherland of China* that hangs in the Island Shangri-La Hotel).**
- The world's largest oceanarium complex **(Ocean Park on the back side of Hong Kong Island).**
- And the city also holds the record for the most money bet annually on horse racing **(at Hong Kong's two horse racing tracks, Happy Valley and Sha Tin).**

And just a few more **"ests"** to finish it up:

- **The beautiful Tsing Ma Bridge is the world's longest road and rail suspension bridge.** Located on the route to the airport, it has six lanes of roadway on the upper deck along with two railroad tracks and two sheltered roadway lanes on the lower deck. And the new 34-mile-long Hong Kong-Zhuhai-Macau bridge is both the longest sea crossing and the longest open-sea fixed link on earth.
- **Hong Kong's Sky City Church**, an international Christian church, holds its services on the **75th floor** of the Central Plaza building on Hong Kong Island. **This gives it the distinction of having the world's highest church within a skyscraper.**
- And, finally, stretching over 2,625 feet, **the Mid-Level escalator on the island is the world's longest outdoor covered escalator system.** Running downhill in the morning and uphill the rest of the day, it provides users with a fascinating glimpse of Hong Kong's bustling lifestyle.

Chinese Term

Abacus

The abacus is an ancient Chinese mathematical device that many have called the world's first computer. Typically made up of a wood or bamboo frame with seven or more vertical rods, it has two moveable beads on each rod in its upper portion and five moveable beads on each rod in its lower portion. The upper area of the abacus is referred to by the Chinese as **heaven** and the lower area is called **earth**. The upper deck beads each have a value of five and the lower ones are each worth one.

In the hands of an **abacist (a person skilled in using an abacus)**, this simple device can quickly perform a number of mathematical operations including addition, subtraction, multiplication, and division – and it can also be used to calculate square roots.

Because of the invention of the hand-held electronic calculator, the use of the abacus in Hong Kong has declined to the point where they are seldom seen any more. However, if you look carefully, you might see them used in a small shop and even sometimes in a bank. Another interesting use of the abacus is by **blind Chinese people**. Many of them find it is a useful tool to help them perform mathematical calculations.

(Note – In 2008, the abacus was listed as **a national Chinese intangible cultural heritage item** by UNESCO. Others on the Chinese intangible cultural heritage list include calligraphy, silk painting, and Chinese opera.)

Moon Gates

A moon gate is a circular opening in a Chinese wall that acts as a passageway for pedestrians. Originally only found in the gardens and homes of wealthy Chinese nobles, moon gates are now common throughout China and are an important element in traditional Chinese architecture. They contain important symbolism for the Chinese and reflect the love they have for the moon.

The Chinese base their traditional calendar on the cycles of the moon. A full moon is a symbol of perfection to them. **It indicates a happy, peaceful, and unified life and any home or garden with a moon gate is thought to be especially desirable.** Whenever the moon is full, the flowers in a garden with a moon gate are considered to be even more beautiful than normal. **Moon gates also symbolize birth, renewal, and a full life.**

Hong Kong has a number of interesting and noteworthy moon gates. Here are a few of my favorites:

- **Lions Pavilion on the Peak** – Just a short walk from the upper terminus of the Peak Tram on Hong Kong Island is a beautiful moon gate that serves as the entryway to the Lions Pavilion lookout area. Through the opening of this moon gate, and from the viewing areas inside the gate, visitors can see the world-renowned panorama of Hong Kong Island, Victoria Harbour, and the Kowloon Peninsula. This view is wonderful at all times of the day, but it is especially nice at sunup, sundown, and in the evening when the lights of the city are on. Travelers have long considered the view of Hong Kong from Victoria Peak to be one of the most spectacular views found anywhere in the world.

- **Kowloon Walled City Park** – A beautiful moon gate serves as one of the entrances to this historic park. Inside the gate, bridges, streams, pagodas, shrubs, and flowers come into view. For several centuries, the Kowloon Walled City served as a military stronghold and protected area for Hong Kong.
- **Po Lin Monastery on Lantau Island** – A beautiful 25-minute cable car ride up a mountain to the Ngong Ping plateau provides access to the wonderful old Po Lin Buddhist Monastery that was founded in 1906. **The monastery has several significant and noteworthy moon gates.** Near the monastery is the remarkable Tian Tan (Big) Buddha located majestically on top of Mount Muk Yue.

- **Tin Hau Temple at Repulse Bay** – Situated on the back side of Hong Kong Island, Repulse Bay is a beautiful and relaxing place to sit on the beach and swim in the South China Sea. On the far southeast end of the beach is a Tin Hau temple complex that has an interesting moon gate. This moon gate is perhaps the most colorful one in Hong Kong with red, yellow, blue, white, and gold elements. While there, also take note of the longevity bridge. **Crossing it is said to add three years to your life.**

- **Ching Shu Hin Along the Ping Shan Heritage Trail** – Located near Yuen Long in the New Territories, this well-preserved building used long ago as a guest house has an interior moon gate that is a wonderful example of old Chinese architecture. Ching Shu Hin is located on the interesting Ping Shan Heritage Trail that includes three villages and 12 historic buildings.

- **Hutong Restaurant on the 28th Floor at #1 Peking Road, Tsim Sha Tsui** – Inside this beautiful award-winning restaurant that serves traditional Northern Chinese cuisine is a beautiful moon gate leading to the restaurant's interior that boasts stunning views of the Kowloon and Hong Kong Island skylines. Signature dishes at Hutong include abalone carpaccio with spring onion oil and scallops tossed with pomelo segments – **or, if you are adventurous, you could try the shark lips marinated with ginger and black fungi!**

- **Hang Mei Tsuen Public Toilet** – For one of the most unique and unusual examples of the use of a moon gate, go to the public toilet building in Hang Mei Tsuen where a moon gate provides access to the restrooms. Hang Mei Tsuen is a housing development located at a light rail stop in the New Territories.

- **Hong Kong Disneyland's Entrance to Space Mountain** – Oh, and perhaps there's one more we could add to the list. How about the entrance to Space Mountain at Hong Kong's Disneyland? **If you use your Disney imagination,** it has the appearance of a moon gate.

And, interestingly, moon gates are also popular in Bermuda. Bermuda is the British island territory located 650 miles east of the U.S. in the North Atlantic. **Bermuda is best known for its Bermuda shorts.** Bermuda shorts are so popular there that it is acceptable to wear them as formal attire to weddings and as business clothing when at work. On these occasions, the shorts are normally worn with knee socks, a tie, and a blazer.

Bermuda has adopted its own version of the moon gate as one of its architectural symbols. The story goes that a Bermudan sea captain saw moon gates on a voyage to China in the late 1800s and fell in love with them. Upon returning home to Bermuda, he set about building his own moon gate. His neighbors and friends loved it and the idea caught on. **The people of Bermuda now believe that a wish made under the arch of a moon gate will come true and that any vows exchanged under moon gates will carry extra happiness and blessings.** It is a common custom today in Bermuda for couples, both locals and tourists, to select places with Chinese moon gates for their weddings.

So, when you visit Hong Kong and other parts of China – as well as Bermuda – **you might want to pay particular attention to moon gates.** Providing a view and entry into a place that has special beauty, meaning, and significance, moon gates are a wonderful architectural feature of many Chinese gardens, homes, and other attractions.

Chinese Term

General Tso

A popular entrée in many Chinese restaurants in the U.S. is **General Tso's Chicken**. Consisting of chunks of chicken that have been dipped in batter and deep fried in a wok, the chicken is then covered with a thick tasty sauce flavored with garlic, scallions, sesame oil, ginger, and hot peppers.

So, who is General Tso and why are we eating his chicken? Chinese history indicates that there was a powerful military leader and statesman known as General Tso during the late Qing dynasty (General Tso was born in 1812 and died in 1885). Although he was a fearless warrior, he had nothing to do with the chicken dish we enjoy so much today. His name was simply borrowed by a modern chef (reportedly one who was working in a Chinese restaurant in New York City in the 1970s) as a catchy name for a dish he had created.

General Tso's Chicken is an example of American Chinese cuisine – food that was developed in America by chefs of Chinese descent. It is a style of cooking that has been adapted to American tastes and which differs somewhat from food found in Hong Kong and mainland China. (In fact, just for fun, I checked the menus of a number of popular Chinese restaurants located in Hong Kong and couldn't find a single one that served General Tso's Chicken.)

Nevertheless, the dish is a big hit in the U.S. **It is so well liked that it is even on the menu in the main mess hall at the U.S. Naval Academy in Annapolis, Maryland.** But they have changed the name a bit to reflect a nautical theme. At the Naval Academy, it is known as **Admiral Tso's Chicken.** No fooling.

Traditional Chinese Medicine

Chinese people in Hong Kong quite often turn to traditional Chinese medicine when a family member is not feeling well. **They do this despite the fact that excellent western medicine and state-of-the-art modern hospitals and clinics are readily available in Hong Kong.** Why do they use traditional Chinese medicine when more modern methods are available to them? Primarily for two reasons: first, because its usage is deeply rooted in Chinese culture and society, and second, because they have found over the centuries that traditional Chinese medicine works quite well in many cases. **Most modern Hong Kongers are practical in nature, and so they often use some of each method, according to the ailment.** They see the two systems of medical practice, traditional Chinese medicine and western medicine, as being complementary to each other – with each one having its strengths and weaknesses.

The foundations of traditional Chinese medicine go back more than 2,500 years. In those days, there existed very little knowledge and understanding of human physiology and anatomy, **so medical practitioners developed the art of observing patients and evaluating the symptoms of sick people by looking at the outside of a person rather than by cutting into them to diagnose and correct a problem.** Over the years, a style of medical treatment was perfected that focuses on five aspects of diagnosis:

1. **Visual** – A detailed observation is made of the face, skin, eyes, and tongue of the patient.

2. **Olfactory** – The various odors emanating from a person are carefully discerned and evaluated.
3. **Auditory** – The sounds a person makes while breathing and moving are studied.
4. **Palpation** – The wrists, abdomen, chest, and other parts of the body are felt to determine the body's rhythms and pulses.
5. **Inquiry** – The patient is asked questions about chills, fever, appetite, thirst, sleep, and pain.

This makes up the entire diagnosis. **No blood tests, x-rays, or heart readings are taken.** When the foregoing steps have been completed by the Chinese doctor, a course of remedies is prescribed for the patient, remedies that typically consist of one or more of the following five items:

Herbal Medicines
If herbal medicines and other natural medicinals are indicated, **which is common**, a long-standing Hong Kong institution comes into play – **the Chinese pharmacy.** Located throughout Hong Kong, Chinese pharmacies are packed from floor to ceiling with container after container of medicinal items. You will see jars, drawers, boxes, and sacks containing hundreds of kinds of dried and preserved herbs, berries, mushrooms, roots, fruits, and vegetables, in addition to all sorts of animal organs, heads, claws, antlers, and fins. **There is hardly a plant, mineral, or animal substance that is not used as a preventative item or a remedy in a Chinese pharmacy.** These hundreds of items can be made into thousands of medicinal concoctions and recipes – all usually done while you wait and observe the action. It is fascinating to watch the pharmacists as they dice, cut, scrape, sort, and weigh everything. The selected items are placed on pieces of paper on the counter and then the papers are carefully folded and tied with string. The customer then carries the packages home where the ingredients are mixed and cooked into a soup, paste, or salve, per the pharmacist's instructions.

An especially interesting location to observe Chinese pharmacies is on Ko Shing Street on Hong Kong Island. **Known as Chinese Medicine Street, Ko Shing Street has the highest concentration of Chinese pharmacies in Hong Kong.** So as to properly control its many traditional Chinese pharmacies and pharmacists, the Hong Kong government has established a **Chinese Medicine Council.** This council regulates the medicines used and sets forth the professional standards for the pharmacists. All traditional Chinese medicine practitioners in Hong Kong are required to meet certain educational standards and pass a licensing exam.

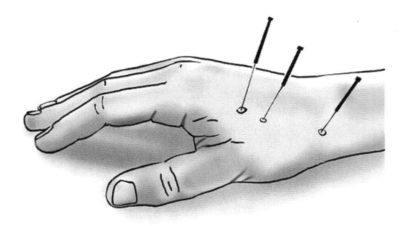

Acupuncture
    Dating back to at least 100 B.C., acupuncture is based on the idea that there are certain neurological pathways that exist in the human body and that inserting a needle at specific points on these pathways and then manipulating the needle can block or stimulate various nerves. Doing so is believed to relieve pain and treat certain diseases. Once thought of as questionable and ineffective, **acupuncture is becoming more accepted worldwide as a complementary approach to conventional treatments, especially for pain.** The World Health Organization believes in acupuncture enough that it maintains a list of diseases and health conditions, most of which are pain and nausea-related in nature, that are possibly treatable by acupuncture. And even TV's **Dr. Oz** has been quoted as saying, "While I wouldn't resort to acupuncture for serious or life-threatening illnesses or wounds, I recommend acupuncture to treat a host of different chronic issues."

Exercise
    Exercise often plays an important role in a Chinese doctor's suggested treatment regimen. A centuries-old form of exercise called t'ai chi ch'uan, **known as tai chi,** is one of the most common ones. It is a Chinese exercise therapy that focuses on breathing and slow movements to enable healing. Tai chi is typically practiced outdoors

in the open air in Hong Kong, either alone or in a group. **It involves continuous gentle dance-like movements that focus on controlling the breathing, relaxing the body, and achieving mental focus.** Sometimes referred to as **meditation in motion,** it is practiced by many people in Hong Kong and is quickly growing in popularity in the western world.

Dietary Therapy

In traditional Chinese medicine, foods also play an important role in treating illnesses. But traditional Chinese doctors don't approach the subject the same as western doctors. For the Chinese doctors, it is not about vitamins, minerals, and recommended daily allowances, rather, it is about reestablishing the body's balance and counteracting the symptoms the body is experiencing by prescribing diets made up of certain classes of foods. **Chinese doctors think more in terms of foods that warm – and foods that cool.** When a patient has a cool illness like fatigue, pallor, anemia, cold feet, sore joints, or stomach pains, warming foods are prescribed to improve circulation and heat up the body. **Warming foods include red meats, deep fried foods, baked goods, squash, onions, nuts, and cherries.** On the other hand, if the patient has rashes, heartburn, perspiration, sore throat, rapid pulse, headaches, etc., cooling foods should be eaten to remove heat and toxins and to calm the blood. **Examples of cooling foods are melons, green vegetables, apples, bananas, bean curd, and eggs.**

Massage

Asian massage is also a commonly prescribed traditional Chinese medicine treatment for certain ailments and illnesses. A relatively gentle form of massage therapy that is typically administered with the person fully clothed, Asian massage is very soothing and relaxing. **Similar to acupuncture in some ways – but without needles – it primarily uses thumb presses, rubbing, gentle percussion, and assisted stretching to promote healing in the body.**

Modern Medical Services in Hong Kong

And just a brief word about what is available in Hong Kong in terms of modern western-style medical services. **In this regard, Hong Kong is first-rate.** Its residents can choose from 12 private hospitals with standards that are on par with the best medical facilities in the western world and 44 public hospitals that are well-equipped and relatively inexpensive. (Typically, a fee of only HK$100 per day

– equal to US$13 – is charged to Hong Kong residents to use the public hospitals.) These excellent facilities, staffed with highly-trained doctors, nurses, and medical staffs, and outfitted with the latest in medical equipment, help to make Hong Kong one of the healthiest places in the world. In fact, based on World Health Organization statistics, **Hong Kong ranks among the best places in the world in both life expectancy (almost 85 years) and infant mortality rate (under three deaths per 1,000).**

So, as a visitor to Hong Kong or as a foreigner residing there, your medical needs will be well taken care of – whether you choose modern medical services or turn to the methods of centuries-old traditional Chinese medicine for your ailments and illnesses. **In Hong Kong, all the bases are covered.**

Chinese Term

Bauhinia

The bauhinia, a type of orchid found in Hong Kong and southeastern China, is the emblem of Hong Kong. Appearing on the Hong Kong flag as a stylized five-petaled white flower on a red background, it is also used on Hong Kong's coins. **Having a pleasant fragrance, the flower of the bauhinia tree is typically white or light pink with crimson highlights.**

The bauhinia flag was first officially hoisted over Hong Kong at 12:01 a.m. on July 1, 1997 as the handover to China took place. Today, a 20-foot-tall sculpture of a golden bauhinia flower is located in Golden Bauhinia Square on Hong Kong Island where the handover ceremony occurred.

Bauhinia is also the radio call sign of **Hong Kong Airlines.**

Runway 13? Oh, No!

Some years ago, when asked which airport in the world was their favorite to land in, a large number of international airline pilots answered that it was Kai Tak, the old airport in Hong Kong. **Kai Tak's Runway 13, and the 47° turn that was required just before touching down,** made it one of the trickiest and most exciting landings anywhere.

Kai Tak Airport, **jutting into Kowloon Bay and Victoria Harbour,** handled Hong Kong's aviation needs from 1925 to 1998. It was closed when the extensive and beautiful new Chek Lap Kok Airport was opened about 20 miles to the west. Although the new airport is much safer and substantially larger, pilots and passengers alike still reminisce about what it was like to come in on approach to Kai Tak and land on Runway 13.

If you've seen Kai Tak, which is now a cruise terminal, you know it was surrounded by rugged mountains, Hong Kong's famous high-rise buildings, and one of the most picturesque harbors in the world. All these things made for unbeatable scenery, **but they presented tricky challenges to pilots trying to land jumbo jets and other aircraft at the airport.** Because of the difficulty of the maneuvers and the skill level required, **most airlines required that the pilot, not a co-pilot, be at the controls during the landing.** Try to picture in your mind the following steps involved in successfully landing a plane at Kai Tak:

1. As the plane approached Hong Kong, it descended, heading in a northeasterly direction.
2. It then flew over the western portion of the crowded harbor.
3. Quickly dropping altitude and speed, the plane passed over the densely populated area of West Kowloon.
4. It then reached a critical visual reference point, **a small hill marked with a large red and white checkerboard pattern on top.** This signaled the beginning of the final approach.
5. Here, less than two nautical miles from touchdown, the pilot was required to make a **47° right turn to line up with the runway.** (The plane typically entered the turn at only about 650 feet of altitude.) This famous turn became known in aviation circles as the **checkerboard turn** or the **Hong Kong turn.**
6. Skimming above the roofs of the tightly packed apartment buildings near the airport, the plane typically exited the turn at about 140 feet of elevation. (The elevation of the runway, which was built on land reclaimed from the harbor, is 28 feet.) **Passengers looking out of the plane's windows could easily see people in their high-rise apartments, the TV shows they were watching, and the laundry they had hung out to dry.** Passengers with nervous dispositions were often advised to avoid looking out the window when coming in for the landing.
7. The pilot then had just a few seconds to fine-tune the approach – i.e. to get to the proper altitude, reduce to the proper speed, and make sure that Runway 13 was indeed directly in front of the plane.
8. Then the plane's wheels would hit the runway **and full brakes would be applied.**

Until 1974, when an instrument guidance system was installed at Kai Tak, **all of this had to be done visually by the pilot and crew,** even at night and in poor weather. The pilots loved Kai Tak's notoriously tricky approach. It gave them an adrenalin rush and tested their skills as a pilot – and most passengers loved it as well, once it was over. Although nearly all planes landed safely over the years, there were a number of them that came in **too high, too low, too fast, too slow, or tilted to one side.** (Note – There are some wonderful videos and photos on the internet showing many of these unsuccessful landings.)

After years of extending the runway further and further into the bay and expanding the airport buildings, Hong Kong finally ran out of room and had to build a new airport to accommodate the tremendous growth in air travel it was experiencing as it became one of the busiest airports in the world.

For any of you who would like to re-experience a Kai Tak landing, or for those of you who haven't done so but would like to see what it was like, go to one of several flight simulator entertainment centers located in Hong Kong or in other cities around the world. (These places provide full-sized actual flight simulators, not video games.) There, for a fee, they will program the Kai Tak approach into their computer and you will be able to sit in the cockpit and use the fully interactive controls of a jumbo jet to attempt a landing at Kai Tak Runway 13. **Video footage of the checkerboard turn will appear outside the cockpit's windows** and you will be required to follow the steps listed above, **including the 47° right turn,** in order to safely land the plane.

When I tried my hand at one of those flight simulators, I failed miserably on each attempted landing. My worst one was when I came in too fast, too high, and crooked **and slid the plane off the end of the runway and into the harbor.** But it was lots of fun trying and brought back great memories of my flights into and out of the old Kai Tak Airport.

Chinese Term

Gung Ho

The phrase **gung ho** is the Anglicized pronunciation of the Chinese term gùnghahp. **It means to be enthusiastic, eager, united, and passionate about a task.** In 1942, a U.S. Marine Major heard the term in China and began using it as a **Marine training slogan.** As used back then by the Chinese, **gung ho** was the shortened name of a Chinese industrial society that emphasized enthusiasm, unity, and harmony. Although first associated in the U.S. with soldiers and warfare, over the years **gung ho** has taken on a much broader usage. Now **gung ho employees** are a plus in an organization, **gung ho athletes** are what most coaches are looking for, and **gung ho students** are the type that teachers hope to have in their classes.

Gung ho has even been used as the name of a popular toy. First released by Mattel in 1983, **Gung-Ho** was a G.I. Joe action figure with a square jaw, huge biceps, and a terrific 6-pack of abdominal muscles.

And the phrase **gung ho** has appeared in films, books, and various enterprises. In 1943, there was a war film released called *Gung Ho!*; in 1986, Ron Howard directed a movie titled *Gung Ho*; there is a **Gung Ho Ministries** in Portland, Oregon; Ken Blanchard published a book in 1997 called *Gung Ho: Turn On the People in Any Organization*; and there's a company called **GungHo Online Entertainment** that produces video games.

Gung ho is a good example of how we have borrowed a term from the Chinese and put it to use in our culture.

Dish Number 27

"**I just love Chinese food. My favorite dish is Number 27.**"
– Clement Attlee, former English Prime Minister

My nephew, Rick, has never been to Hong Kong. When I asked him if he would like to travel there, he said that he didn't have much desire to go because he didn't think he would like the food. To quote him, **"If I can't say the name or recognize the food, it freaks me out."** So, this chapter is dedicated to Rick (and others who have similar feelings about foreign food) in an attempt to point out the many wonderful and safe food choices there are in the modern cosmopolitan city of Hong Kong. Sure, there is food you can't pronounce and don't recognize, but there's also a wide array of cuisine that most everyone would be comfortable with.

Hong Kong is a food-obsessed culture and no other city boasts quite as eclectic a dining scene as Hong Kong. Eating places range from the most opulent restaurants with celebrity chefs to the humblest of eateries. Food is vitally important to the Chinese. An old Chinese adage says, **"Eating is more important than the emperor,"** and Confucius said, **"All chefs must perform their trade with exactness. Cooks must strive for perfection."** With this long tradition of emphasis on food, no wonder Hong Kong has so many excellent restaurants and such great cuisine.

Some of my most pleasant memories of Hong Kong are related to the food I have eaten there, so one of the reasons I love to return often is to eat great Hong Kong meals. I personally love Chinese food, but it is not just the Chinese cuisine that is a highlight to me, but also the many other types of excellent food available in this remarkable city. **Regardless of your food tastes or budget, there is no reason to be nervous about eating in Hong Kong.**

The majority of Hong Kongers have ties to the Canton (Guangdong) region of southern China, so Cantonese-style food is the most widely available cuisine there. Using stir frying, roasting, steaming, and braising, Cantonese food is a diverse cuisine known for its freshness and vast array of seasonings and flavors. Because Hong Kong people work long hours and have such a fast-paced life, eating out is common and so there are restaurants everywhere in this densely packed and hectic city. Let's discuss some of the cuisine options available.

Local Hong Kong-Style Food

Large Cantonese Restaurants – Hong Kong is full of large Chinese restaurants with vast menus of Cantonese specialties. **Meals are almost always eaten with family and friends around large circular tables.** Ordering is done as a group, with everyone sharing the food as it is brought to the table. Soup is usually served first. **Then a vast array of dishes featuring pork, chicken, beef, and fish are provided. Rice is always part of the meal.** Dessert, although not as common as in western cuisine, can range from fresh seasonal fruits to tofu pudding. Meals last a long time and are quite noisy affairs. Everyone talks and has a great time visiting with each other. **Recommendations** – The Jumbo Floating Restaurant in Aberdeen harbor and the Dynasty Restaurant in Wan Chai have strong reputations. Also, make time to eat dim sum while you are in Hong Kong. Served in the late morning and early afternoon, dim sum is a Hong Kong tradition.

Seafood Restaurants – Some of my favorite places to eat in Hong Kong are the restaurants specializing in seafood. Most of them have large fish tanks visible as you enter the restaurant. **You just point out the particular fish you would like, and within minutes it will be on your table, prepared and seasoned to your exact order.** A favorite way to prepare fish in Hong Kong is to steam the whole fish, including the head, and dress it in peanut oil, soy sauce, coriander, and chives. Although the seafood restaurants in the city are excellent, an enjoyable thing to do is to travel by ferry to some of the outlying islands where you can enjoy fresh-as-can-be seafood served at your table overlooking the water. **Recommendations** – The China Star Seafood Restaurant in Tsim Sha Tsui and the Rainbow Seafood Restaurant in Sok Kwu Wan on Lamma Island are excellent.

Small Hole-in-the-Wall Restaurants – Tucked into every imaginable place in Hong Kong are small restaurants serving wonderful local food. Much of the food consists of stewed and steamed items. **Dumplings, noodles, and barbecued meats are favorites.** Sharing a table with others you do not know is common during busy hours. **Recommendations** – Head to Hennessy Road in the Causeway Bay area on the island and to Shui Wah Street in Kwun Tong on the Kowloon side.

Open-Air Stalls – Small out-in-the-open stalls specializing in fish balls, noodles, and meat snacks of all kinds are widely popular in Hong Kong. **They are fast and cheap,** and if you are careful and stick with hot items freshly cooked, the food should be safe to eat. All eateries in Hong Kong, including the small ones, are regulated by the Hong Kong Food and Environmental Hygiene Department and are inspected regularly. **Recommendations** – Go to Temple Street in Mong Kok and to Tsuen Wan in the New Territories.

Street Vendors – Called hawkers, street vendors provide the most adventurous part of eating in Hong Kong. **My nephew should probably avoid these.** Usually working from push carts, street vendors specialize in a variety of foods, particularly deep fried dishes. Unusual foods like marinated pig's ear, stinky tofu, and fried squid tentacles are some of the popular offerings available from street vendors. **Recommendations** – Try the area around Ladies Street in Mong Kok in the evening and go to Wan Chai on the island any time.

Bakeries – Hong Kong's bakeries are terrific. Try their **bolo bau pineapple buns** (my personal favorite bakery item), **egg tarts** (my wife's favorite), and their many **cakes. Recommendations** – Try the bakeries located in the malls and inside the MTR stations.

Other Chinese and Asian Cuisines

Szechuan (or Sichuan) Chinese – Szechuan, a large province in southwest China, is known for adding hot spices to their dishes by using **liberal amounts of chilies and peppercorns.** Kung pao chicken, twice-cooked pork, and spicy noodles are popular Szechuan dishes. **Recommendations** – San Xi Lou in Central on the island and Chuan Shao in Kowloon.

Beijing and Northern Chinese – Along with rice, wheat is common in northern China, so restaurants in Hong Kong offering Beijing and northern Chinese cuisine feature lots of breads, pancakes, and pastries. **Lamb is popular and Peking duck is a much-sought-after delicacy worth going out of your way for.** Some of the dishes are rather exotic and require advance ordering. **Recommendations** – Peking Garden in Star House near the Star Ferry terminal on the Kowloon side and the Northern Chinese Restaurant in Quarry Bay on the island.

Chiu Chow Chinese – Known for its vegetarian and seafood dishes, Chiu Chow items are mostly poached, steamed, or braised. Fish ball noodle soup and non-fried spring rolls are popular. **Recommendations** – The Chiu Chow Garden Restaurant in Tai Koo on the island and the Chong Fat Restaurant in Kowloon City.

Hunan Chinese – With spicy flavors, Hunan cuisine's cooking methods feature stewing, frying, and smoking. Braised pork, steamed fish, and spicy eggplant in garlic sauce are favorites.

Recommendations – Café Hunan in Kowloon and Hu Nan Heen in Causeway Bay on the island.

Other Asian – Hong Kong has terrific Japanese, Indian, Malaysian, Thai, Vietnamese, and Nepalese restaurants. Sushi in Hong Kong is excellent, as is Indian curry, Malaysian satay, and Mongolian hot pot. **Recommendations** – For Japanese food head to Causeway Bay on the island, for Indian go to Tsim Sha Tsui in Kowloon, and for Thai visit Kowloon City.

Vegetarian – With the high number of Hong Kong residents following Buddhism, vegetarian restaurants are common. They have tasty ways to fix tofu, wheat gluten, mushrooms, and vegetables. **Some of the dishes can taste and look almost identical to real meat.** **Recommendations** – For a special vegetarian meal experience, eat at the Po Lin Monastery on Lan Tau Island at the foot of the Big Buddha and for a good vegetarian restaurant in the city, try Happy Veggies in Wan Chai on Hong Kong Island.

Western and European Food

Having been an important center for world commerce for decades and a very popular tourist destination, Hong Kong has a large number of excellent restaurants serving western-style and European-style cuisine. **Many of these restaurants have world-renowned chefs, beautiful décor, and top-of-the-line menu items.** Some of the best French, Italian, American, British, Spanish, German, Turkish, Greek, and Russian food you'll find anywhere in the world is available in Hong Kong. **Recommendations** – Go to the restaurants in the better hotels on both the Hong Kong and Kowloon side. They have excellent menus and offer terrific western and European food! Or enjoy lunch or an evening meal at one of the many restaurants at Knutsford Terrace, a pedestrian-only street in Tsim Sha Tsui on the Kowloon side. Or go to the array of fine restaurants on Elgin Street near the top of the Mid-Level escalator on the island.

Fast Food

Hong Kong is highly westernized, so United States-style fast food is common. **McDonald's is everywhere, as is Pizza Hut, and KFC.** You'll also find Burger King, Popeyes, Subway, and even Häagen Dazs. And Chinese-style fast food outlets with delicious local food have also sprung up (think of a Burger King-type place serving noodles topped with pork cutlets and gravy). Fast food places for all tastes are everywhere throughout Hong Kong. **Recommendations** – Go to the food courts at Hong Kong's gigantic indoor malls, such as Festival Walk in Kowloon Tong or New Town Plaza in Sha Tin in the New Territories. For Chinese-style fast food, look for Café de Coral and Fairwood eateries throughout the city.

Miscellaneous Hong Kong Food Thoughts

Appearance – Especially in Hong Kong, it is important not to judge a book by its cover. **Some of the most unassuming places to eat provide the best meals.** Luxurious restaurants and simple eateries often sit right next to each other.

Chinese Food Take-Out Boxes – In Hong Kong, you won't often find the type of take-out boxes we get at Chinese restaurants in the U.S. They're more of a western invention. And the same goes with fortune cookies. They are not handed out in Chinese restaurants in Hong Kong.

Great November Feast – Every year since 2009, Hong Kong has presented an event called the **Great November Feast.** It is an entire month of gourmet happenings, food fairs, and discounts at restaurants. One of the main locations for the festivities is at the harborfront in Central where you can visit dozens of booths offering tasty snacks and experience live music and entertainment while eating.

Food Tasting Tours – Supported by the Hong Kong Tourism Board, a variety of food tasting tours are offered throughout the year. Called **Hong Kong Foodie Tasting Tours,** the price of the ticket allows you to go with a certified food guide to visit six restaurants in a particular area of Hong Kong. Tours include visits to some of the kitchens. More than just being tasting tours, the knowledgeable guides make them historical and cultural experiences as well.

So, Rick, one of the hallmarks of Hong Kong is its wide variety of wonderful food to suit just about every taste. Besides enjoying the fascinating and unique sights of Hong Kong, **I'm betting you'd like the food there and that Hong Kong would be the kind of place you would want to return to often.** It's really a great place to visit. And if you're not sure what to order, just ask for **Dish Number 27.**

"The Chinese have been cooking for more than 5,000 years, so their culinary arts are further along the evolutionary cooking chain than cheeseburgers."
– Anonymous

Chinese Term

Cantopop

Cantopop, a type of music that originated in Hong Kong, **uses Cantonese words set to popular music** instead of Mandarin words. Combining the words "Cantonese" and "popular," Cantopop is a genre that has spread throughout Asia and wherever Hong Kong people live. Like our own musical celebrities, **Cantopop performers are idolized by their Hong Kong fans.** Especially popular in the 1980s and 1990s, **there is presently a Cantopop resurgence taking place in Hong Kong.**

If you're looking to experience a modern and trendy aspect of Hong Kong's culture, you might consider getting tickets to a Cantopop concert at the Hong Kong Coliseum or the AsiaWorld-Arena. Take some earplugs.

Lucky Number 8

From the day they come into the world until the time they pass on to the next one, gathering lucky numbers is a way of life for many of the people of Hong Kong. **They believe that lucky numbers bring good fortune, are a good omen, lead to success, and bode well for the future.** A Hong Kong person's faith in these lucky numbers is found everywhere – from choosing on which floor of a building they will live, which license plate number to place on their car, and which airplane flight to select. Conversely, certain numbers are unlucky in their culture and Chinese people in Hong Kong go to great lengths to avoid them.

Although there are some differing opinions among the Chinese themselves concerning the degree of luckiness and unluckiness of certain numbers, **most in Hong Kong view the number 8 as the luckiest number and 4 as the unluckiest one.** This is because when it is spoken, **the number 8 sounds similar to the word for prosperity and wealth.** Similarly, the number four is thought to be very unlucky because **it sounds like the word for death.** (Words like these that sound alike but have different meanings we call homophones. In English, blue and blew are homophones, as are flower and flour.)

In this chapter, let's take a look at some examples of how these two numbers – **the very lucky number 8 and the very unlucky number 4** – come into play in Hong Kong life.

- **License Plates** – Since 1973, the Hong Kong government has auctioned off lucky license plate numbers rather than assign them out on a random basis. The proceeds of the auctions go to various charities in Hong Kong. **Any license plate with an 8 in it is much sought after and goes for a premium.** If a plate with multiple 8s comes up at the auction, huge sums are bid for it. (One of the highest amounts ever paid for a lucky license plate was in excess of HK$5 million, or more than US$640,000.) One of the most prestigious things a person in Hong Kong can do is to drive a luxury automobile with a lucky license plate number on it.

- **Floor Numbers** – The way floors are numbered and the price people pay to be on those floors in Hong Kong's high-rise buildings reflect their belief about lucky and unlucky

numbers. **Floors such as 8, 18, 28, etc. are lucky, and prices and rents charged to be on those levels are higher than on other floors.** (Real estate agents say that they can get as much as a 20% premium for those floors.) If a building goes up as high as 88 floors (**88 represents double good fortune**), and you could get an apartment or an office on that floor, look out. That level in the building would be considered extremely auspicious and would cost substantially more than normal. So, despite the extra rental cost, the Hong Kong Monetary Authority, one of Hong Kong's most influential and important government agencies, **chose the lucky 88th floor of the International Finance Centre building on Hong Kong island for its headquarters.** Also, the number 4 is often avoided in the numbering of floors. There might not be a 4th, 14th, 24th, etc. floor in the building. (They also might avoid a 13th floor because of the many westerners who live in Hong Kong who consider 13 to be unlucky.) So, for instance, let's say that there is a building in Hong Kong where the top floor in the building is called floor #50. **That building might not actually have 50 floors.** It might have fewer than that if the developer chose to skip the floors with the number 4 in them – and also the 13th floor.

- **Weddings** – On his wedding day, Chinese custom is for the groom to give money to the sisters of the bride and the bridesmaids as he picks up the bride. The amounts of money given by the groom are often multiples of 8 – **like HK$88 or HK$888** – to help ensure that the marriage will be a lucky one that lasts long and is filled with good fortune.

- **Telephone Numbers** – Any phone number with an 8 in it, or with several 8s, is very desirable – and those with 4s in them are avoided. Let's say you want to get hold of the boss of a company without having to go through the telephone receptionist. **Just try extension 8 or 88 and see what happens.** Most likely, the luckiest extension number in the company has been taken by the boss.

- **Product Pricing** – In the west, we like to use 9s in the price of our products (such as US$2.99 for a gallon of gas and US$13.99 for a large pizza). In Hong Kong, they use 8s (HK$8.80 for a lychee-flavored candy bar and HK$288.80 for an electric rice cooker). **Hong Kong is full of items with 8s in their price and not often would you see something sold for a price that has a lot of 4s in it.**

- **Path to Enlightenment** – The Buddhists follow the **Noble Eightfold Path** in their search for enlightenment and spiritual liberation.

- **Numbering Products** – When companies come out with new versions of their products, it is often the practice to number the models consecutively. **But many savvy companies have been known to skip version 4 when putting their product into the Hong Kong market.** An example of this is Canon cameras. In Asia, their PowerShot G series has a G3X model and a G5X model, but not a G4X model, and Nokia cell phones have avoided placing a 4 in the product number of their Lumia phones. Similarly, companies look for opportunities to put the number 8 into the products they sell in China. For instance, the General Motors minivan that is sold in the Chinese market is called the Buick GL8 (for Good Luck 8). No such model is sold in other countries. And Chinese restaurants all over the world have a special soup on their menus called **Eight Treasures Soup.**

- **Summer Olympic Games** – China eagerly went after the rights to host the 2008 summer Olympics. Once they were awarded those games, **they scheduled the opening ceremony for 8/8/08 and set the starting time to be precisely at 8 minutes and 8 seconds after 8 o'clock in the evening local time.** This strategy worked out extremely well. The games were very successful, with China doing the best they had ever done in an Olympics, winning 98 total medals – 58% more than they had ever won before.

- **Airline Flights** – Not by accident, one of Cathay Pacific's daily flights from Hong Kong to Vancouver is **Flight #CX888** and KLM's flight from Hong Kong to Amsterdam is **Flight #KL888.** Any airlines that are aware of how the Chinese view numbers, typically avoid placing a 4 in the flight number of any of their planes going into or coming out of Hong Kong.

- **Passwords and PINs** – If you are ever trying to figure out the password or PIN of a Chinese person, **you might want to try one with lots of 8s in it.** They love using 8s in their identification numbers.

- **Disneyland Hotel Ballroom** – The huge main ballroom at the Disneyland Hotel at Hong Kong's Disneyland Resort measures **888 square meters.**

- **Dates for Important Events** – The primary influence in picking dates for important events in Hong Kong is feng shui, **but a secondary factor in setting dates is this lucky number thing.** Weddings on the 8th day of the month are auspicious, opening a new store on the 8th is a good omen, and having a baby born on the 8th brings good fortune to both the parents and the child.
- **Bank Accounts** – Bank accounts and bank services with lots of 8s in them are valued. Several years ago, when a Hong Kong bank opened a new branch office in Kowloon, three of their safety deposit boxes – **the ones numbered 8, 88, and 888** – were raffled off for extra money to the highest bidders.

As can be seen, to many of the people of Hong Kong the number 8 is much sought after whereas the number 4 is to be avoided. **While some Chinese do this number thing just for fun, many believe seriously in it and tailor a good deal of their day-to-day actions and decisions accordingly.**

So, you might ask to what extent I personally buy into this lucky number idea. **Well…somewhat, but not completely.** I did choose to make this chapter about lucky numbers **Chapter 8** in the book, but if I wholeheartedly believed in Chinese lucky vs. unlucky numbers, **I would have published this book on August 8, it would have 88 pages, there would be no chapter 4, 14, or 24, and the book would sell for HK$88.88 or US$8.88.**

(Note – If you'd like to delve further into how the Chinese culture views the entire subject of lucky numbers, the book *Chinese Numbers* by Evelyn Lip is an interesting read.)

Chinese Term

Stinky Tofu

Does stinky tofu really stink? **The answer is a resounding YES!** It absolutely stinks. The smell of stinky tofu being deep fried by a vendor on the streets of Hong Kong is horrible! Interestingly enough, though, the taste of stinky tofu is not so bad. And because of its high protein content, it is a very healthy food.

Stinky tofu is bean curd that has sat around in brine for much too long. Having become fermented, it emanates a rotten smell when fried, but when covered with red chili sauce or soy sauce after being cooked, it becomes a popular Cantonese treat.

I find it interesting that street vendors in Hong Kong actually try to outdo their competitors by amping up their culinary skills to see who can produce the smelliest tofu – all so they can attract more business. **Go figure.**

Chinese Ancestry

"To forget one's ancestors is to be a brook without a source, a tree without a root." – Chinese Proverb

As you know, there are a lot of people in China. At the exact moment that I am starting to write this chapter, **the population of China is estimated by the Worldometer population counter to be 1,437,222,061 – over 1.4 billion people.** With approximately **18.5%** of the earth's humans, China is the most populous country in the world. In fact, if you were to consider the five largest provinces of China to be separate countries (Guangdong, Shandong, Henan, Sichuan, and Jiangsu), **they by themselves would each rank in the world's top 20 countries in population.**

China is not only the most populous country at the present time, it has been the most populous one in the world for many centuries. As a result, if you look at the total number of people who have lived on the earth during its entire history **(which is estimated by the Population Reference Bureau to be 108 billion people)** the Chinese would make up by far the largest group.

With so many ancestors, it is no wonder that the people of Hong Kong love genealogy and family history and are passionate about tracing their roots and learning about their ancestors. There are a number of resources available to them to do so.

Jiapu

Jiapu are Chinese family genealogy books. In these books, the village birthplace and burial site for each male relative is listed. **Interestingly, Jiapu normally trace the male lineage of the family or clan, not the female lineage.** Wives and daughters are sometimes listed, but matriarchal lines are not usually traced.

These books are fascinating, but because much of the information is written in centuries-old Chinese characters, many modern Chinese people find them somewhat difficult to decipher and read. Jiapu are often located in ancestral halls and ancestral villages, or they might be in the possession of the eldest son in a family line.

Genealogical experts indicate that the longest substantiated pedigree in the world is the one for the great Chinese sage Confucius. Going back more than 2,500 years, his record is now up to 85 generations – and counting. According to the **Confucius Genealogy Compilation Committee** (yes, there really is such a thing), Confucius has at least 3 million descendants.

Ancestral Halls

Ancestral halls have been erected by the Chinese for centuries. They are not devoted to a particular religion or belief, **rather they are dedicated to a specific clan or family.** The halls contain ancestral tablets and other important family treasures and are a frequent gathering place for family members. **A good example in Hong Kong of one of these is the Tang Clan Ancestral Hall in the Fan Ling area of the New Territories. It is a 700-hundred-year-old structure that is one of Hong Kong's oldest historical monuments.** Open to the public on most days of the year, it is a fascinating place to visit.

Inside this wonderful old structure, you will find more than 100 family ancestral tablets, arranged by seniority and placed on a tiered altar along the rear wall of the innermost chamber. **Each tablet is a memorial to a specific ancestor whose name is engraved and painted in gold on it.** As is customary, only men's tablets are included. Ancestral halls are a great source of pride to clan members and provide excellent family history information.

Excursion to One's Ancestral Village

Because China has primarily been an agrarian society for most of its history, family units are closely tied to the land the family owned and worked for generations in their ancestral village. **Therefore, the ancestral home and birthplace of the family plays an important social role in each Chinese person's identity.** As Chinese people meet and get acquainted with each other for the first time, an important question they often ask each other is what their ancestral home is. (And, when they do so, it should be remembered that the ancestral home in question is that of their father, not their mother.) A life-long goal of many Hong Kong Chinese is to make a trip to their ancestral village. A number of travel companies, such as My China Roots, specialize in organizing these trips and providing expert guides to accompany you on your visit.

Libraries and Online Resources

Great amounts of Chinese ancestral information are available by visiting various libraries in person and accessing online websites. Several of the largest and best Chinese family history resources are:

- **The Fung Ping Shan Library at the University of Hong Kong** – The oldest university in Hong Kong and one of Asia's most prestigious educational institutions, the University of Hong Kong has an impressive collection of Chinese histories and genealogies in its Fung Ping Shan Library. Access to the library is free.

- **Shanghai Library Jiapu Database** – The largest collection of Chinese genealogical materials in the world is the Shanghai Library's jiapu database, which is free to the public. Their website and searchable database are extensive and amazing – but the information is written only in Chinese. There is no English translation available.

- **The Family History Library in Salt Lake City, Utah** – Operated by The Church of Jesus Christ of Latter-day Saints, this facility is the largest genealogical library in the world. It contains a vast number of family records and documents, including millions from China. Representatives of the library have been in China for a number of years photographing and digitizing Chinese family records for the library's database. All of the information and resources of the Family History Library are free. To create an account and gain access to the information contained in the library, go to FamilySearch.org.

Last-Minute Update

In keeping with my desire to be as accurate as possible in this book, I need to update the population number for China. **During the time (a little over 90 minutes) it has taken me to write a rough draft of this chapter, the population of China has grown to 1,437,223,107, an increase of 1,046 people.**

"Consider the past and you shall know the future."
– Chinese Proverb

Chinese Term

Middle Kingdom

In Chinese, the name of China literally means **middle kingdom** or central state. They have referred to their country in this manner for many centuries. By doing so they weren't trying to be arrogant, they were just stating their belief, according to their knowledge of the world at the time, that they were in the center of civilization and in the middle of the world they were familiar with.

A type of map called the **Wangou Qiantu** world map reflects this idea. It shows China located near the center of the map with Europe and Africa to the left and the Americas to the right.

The Hungry Ghost and Other Festivals

Some of my favorite times in Hong Kong have been during Chinese festivals. With five major festivals, along with a number of quaint and interesting minor ones, **it seems like there is always something going on in Hong Kong to entertain you and to help you experience Chinese culture first hand.**

Minor Festivals

The Hungry Ghost Festival

The **Hungry Ghost Festival** is an event that I find very interesting. Celebrated on the fifteenth day of the seventh month of the lunar calendar, it's the time of the year when ghosts come out from the lower realm to pay everyone a visit. **The ghosts can be wonderfully friendly and helpful if they are properly taken care of, but if they are ignored or abused, horrible luck will ensue.** The ghosts love to be entertained, so elaborate and loud Chinese opera and other musical programs are presented for them on large stages erected in various parks around Hong Kong.

If you attend a performance, be careful not to sit in any of the empty front row seats that have the special red coverings on them. **These seats are for the ghosts, and they get very angry if their chair is taken.** The ghosts have extravagant tastes, so wonderful meals are prepared for them and lots of fake paper money, automobiles, servants, and mansions are burned so they will have these things when they return to the lower realm.

Da Siu Yan Festival (Villain Hitting Festival)

And how about the **Da Siu Yan Festival,** one of the most practical and helpful celebrations of them all? **Da siu yan means to hit little people.** Elderly Chinese ladies sit on short Chinese stools underneath the Canal Road flyover in Causeway Bay waiting for you to hire them to hit someone who has wronged you or to direct some bad luck to one of your enemies. They do this by hitting a photograph you provide of your enemy (or a piece of paper with the name of your enemy written on it) **with the sole of an old shoe. It is a riot to watch them flail away at the person you have paid them to get even with.**

Lam Tsuen Wishing Festival

And one more minor festival worth checking out is the **Lam Tsuen Wishing Festival.** Held during the same time as Chinese New Year in the village of Lam Tsuen in the New Territories, it is an occasion where you write your wishes on a piece of red or gold paper that is tied to one end of a string. **An orange is tied to the other end of the string and then the orange and the wish are thrown up into the wishing tree. If the orange and the wish stay in the tree, the wish will be granted.**

Up until a few years ago, a special live wishing tree was used, but as the festival grew in popularity, the weight of the many oranges threatened to harm the tree. So now the written wishes are thrown onto an imitation tree. This is a lively and colorful festival that includes great quantities of food, cultural performances, game booths, beautiful decorations, and **lighted wishing lanterns** that are placed on little boats that are set afloat in the evenings on the Lam Tsuen canal. The whole celebration spans several weeks and is a lot of fun.

Major Festivals

In addition to these and other smaller festivals, **there are five major festivals in Hong Kong,** with each one celebrated as a public holiday. They help make Hong Kong a fascinating place to visit and an enjoyable city in which to live.

Chinese New Year

Chinese New Year, also known as the Spring Festival, begins on the eve of the first day of the first lunar month. **It is the granddaddy of all Hong Kong festivals, being by far the most colorful and important one.** The first three days of the 15-day festival are statutory public holidays for the people of Hong Kong. Chinese New Year is a time to honor ancestors and deities and is celebrated by cleaning the house (in order to sweep away bad fortune), settling old debts, gathering the family, feasting, watching parades (the lion and dragon dancing are highlights), setting off firecrackers (now banned except for government-sponsored fireworks displays over the harbor), decorating homes and shops with red signs and banners (red symbolizes joy, luck, and prosperity), and paying generous bonuses to employees.

Adults give unmarried children red envelopes called lai see that contain newly minted money. **The familiar new year greeting kung hei fat choi is said constantly to everyone you see and is roughly translated to mean may you be lucky and get rich.** Chinese New Year starts on the following dates in coming years:

- 2021 – February 12, the year of the ox
- 2022 – February 1, the year of the tiger
- 2023 – January 22, the year of the rabbit

The Chinese zodiac runs on a 12-year cycle. The twelve zodiac animals are rat, ox, tiger, rabbit, dragon, snake, horse, goat, monkey, rooster, dog, and pig. **I was born in the year of the dog and my wife was born in the year of the tiger.** As a dog, I am loyal, kind, temperamental, and determined. As a tiger, Holly is brave, charming, intelligent, and generous. And you? Do you know what animal you are and what your traits are?

Ching Ming Festival (Tomb Sweeping Day)

The Ching Ming Festival comes on the 15th day after the spring equinox (usually around April 4). **Ching Ming translates to clean and bright,** and it is on this day that the Chinese go to the burial grounds of their ancestors to clean the graves. The cleaning often entails sweeping the graves, weeding around them, touching up the headstone inscriptions, making food and other offerings, and lighting incense. It is quite a sight to observe thousands upon thousands of Chinese as they pack the cemeteries of Hong Kong to pay homage to their ancestors. **(Think U.S. Memorial Day times two or three.)** Hong Kong has numerous cemeteries, but one that is especially interesting to visit during Ching Ming is the Chai Wan Permanent Cemetery on a huge hillside above Chai Wan, which is towards the east side of Hong Kong Island.

And an interesting thing has developed in recent years relating to making offerings to ancestors. In the past, the most popular offerings to burn at the tomb were fake cash, paper homes, and paper servants. **Now, however, you'll also see people burn paper imitations of modern conveniences such as mobile phones, laptops, flat screen TVs, video games, sports cars, air conditioners, designer handbags, etc.**

Dragon Boat Festival

A great spectator festival is the Dragon Boat Festival, also known as Tuen Ng. Held in a number of harbors around Hong Kong on the 5th day of the 5th lunar month (in May or June), **this is when dragon boats full of paddlers race each other.** (Smaller boats hold as few as 20 and the largest ones might have as many as 80 paddlers.) Each canoe-like boat, which has a dragon's head carved into the bow and a dragon's tail carved into the stern, carries a crew of paddlers as well as a drummer who sets the timing for the paddle strokes by beating a huge drum set in the boat. Although all of the race locations are wonderful places to watch the festivities, I personally prefer to go to the Aberdeen Harbour on the back side of the island. Boisterous crowds line the shores of the venues to cheer on their favorite rowing clubs and organizations, making for quite an outdoor party.

Along with the boat races, another popular part of the Dragon Boat Festival is the eating of **steamed glutinous rice dumplings called zongzi.** Wrapped in large bamboo leaves and stuffed with fillings such as black bean paste, pork with chestnuts, and salted duck eggs, zongzi dumplings are delicious.

The Dragon Boat Festival commemorates the death of the ancient Chinese scholar and poet Chu Yuan. **After being banished for treason, he threw himself into the Miluo River.** The local people greatly admired the poet, so they set out on the river in boats to find and rescue him. They beat drums and threw balls of sticky rice into the river in hopes that the sound of the drums would scare away any fish that might eat Chu Yuan and that the fish that weren't frightened by the drums would eat the dumplings instead of him. Although their attempts failed, their boats and their dumplings are commemorated each year during the Dragon Boat Festival.

Mid-Autumn Festival (Moon Festival)

An old Chinese saying shared with family members during the **Mid-Autumn Festival** held in September or early October each year (on the 15th day of the 8th lunar month) is, **"May we live long and share the beauty of the moon together."** Held when the moon is believed to be the fullest and roundest of the year, the Mid-Autumn Festival, or **Moon Festival,** is a time to celebrate the end of the harvest season. Believing in the power of the moon to rejuvenate and bless, families gather together and give mooncakes to each other to show appreciation for the good fortune they have received during the year.

Mooncakes are round pastries about four inches in diameter and about one-and-three-quarter inches thick that are filled with a lotus seed paste or bean paste wrapped around a salty egg yolk. Mooncakes are very sweet and very dense – and not everyone likes them – but the people of Hong Kong love to give them to each other as presents.

Representing the full autumn moon, **brightly lit lanterns in beautiful colors** are hung in trees and paraded around Hong Kong's parks by numerous children. Dragon dances and lion dances are another big part of the Mid-Autumn Festival celebration. **One of the best dragon dances is the fire dragon dance performed in Tai Hang in Causeway Bay on the island.** Here, an unusually lengthy dragon made of straw and covered with burning incense sticks, winds its way through the back streets of Tai Hang, accompanied by loud drumming. The dragon emits a great amount of smoke and there is lots of noise during the several hours it performs. To see it best, go early and find a spot on Wun Sha Street.

Chung Yeung Festival

The **Chung Yeung Festival** comes in October on the 9th day of the 9th lunar month. **It is a time to go to the outdoors to picnic, fly kites, and climb high mountains.** (Hong Kong's tallest mountain is 3,140-foot Tai Mo Shan in the New Territories while the Peak on Hong Kong Island is 1,811 feet high.) Climbing mountains and flying kites are believed to be methods of driving away danger and of carrying bad luck away from you and your family. **It is also a day to visit graves,** similar to what is done in the spring during the Ching Ming Festival. As you can tell, with two major festivals involving the graves of ancestors, Hong Kong's cemeteries get lots of TLC and paying respect to the departed is an important part of Chinese culture.

Chinese Term

Erhu

The erhu (pronounced **yìhwùh** in Cantonese) is a two-stringed Chinese musical instrument. In the hands of an expert musician, it is an amazing instrument that can produce a wide variety of music – **from melancholic tunes, to lively melodies, and even to sounds that are similar to the human voice.**

With a vertical neck about 32 inches long, the erhu has two tuning pegs at the top and a small hexagonally shaped sound box at the bottom which is often made from aged rosewood, sandalwood, or ebony. The sound box is normally covered with snake skin from a python. The two playing strings are made of twisted silk, nylon, or metal and the bow string is made of horse hair. **A unique aspect of playing the erhu is that the musician changes the pitch and sound of the strings by touching the strings with the fingers and not by pushing the strings against the neck of the instrument as is done in playing a violin or guitar. There is no fingerboard.** Also, the bow is never totally separated from the strings. Instead, the bow hair passes between the two playing strings, going over one and under the other. As a result, the bow cannot be removed from the instrument without undoing the playing string it goes under.

If you have the chance while in Hong Kong, you might enjoy attending a performance of the **Hong Kong Chinese Orchestra.** Made up of approximately 85 musicians, including ten to twelve who play the erhu, all of the orchestra's instruments are traditional Chinese ones that produce music that has quite a different sound than that of a western symphony orchestra.

And perhaps without realizing it you heard erhus if you attended **Cirque du Soleil's *"O"*** while you were in Las Vegas. Presented at the Bellagio, **that very popular show's music features the erhu.**

Mission Hills 216

When I first lived in Hong Kong some 50 years ago, **Hong Kong was a British Crown Colony** and it had two golf courses, one on the island and one in the New Territories. I don't recall knowing of any golf courses located in mainland China at that time. Under the rule of Chairman Mao, the Chinese viewed golf as **an evil bourgeois pastime** and they steered clear of it. In fact, the government banned it.

When we went back to Hong Kong in 2006 to live there for three years, things had changed. Hong Kong had been handed back to China by the British, and China was into golf big time. Hong Kong itself had seven golf courses and **the largest golf complex in the entire world sat just over the Hong Kong border in Shenzhen, China.** That golf complex is called **Mission Hills 216** and I have been fortunate to play it twice – once on the Olazabal course and once on the Els course.

Mission Hills is amazing. **It consists of 12 full-sized courses all in one location.** The beautiful courses have been designed by an array of famous golf personalities – **Olazabal, Els, Sorenstam, Nicklaus, Dye, Faldo, etc.** The central club house, one of three clubhouses in the complex, is a spectacular 300,000 square-foot show place with the largest pro shop in the world. The courses are well-groomed, the staff is extremely friendly, and if you didn't know any better you'd think you were golfing at a premier country club in the U.S. Mission Hills has a five-star resort hotel, a world-class spa, a huge top-of-the-line shopping mall, and the largest tennis center in Asia.

Because golf was brought to China from other countries, and because China uses characters for their written language rather than an alphabet, the word "golf" and the words associated with playing golf don't exist in their language. **So they have transliterated those words.** That means they have chosen sounds from their language and have used those sounds to approximate the English way of saying the word. They do this all the time with foreign words that don't exist in Chinese. Here are some examples of transliterated golf words in the Cantonese Chinese language that have been spelled out in what is called Romanization:

- **golf** – gōyíhfū
- **ball** – bō
- **birdie** – bōdí
- **caddie** – gàdí
- **cup** – kàp

Today, China is struggling with golf as a pastime. **They can't quite make up their mind about it.** When the communist government came into power in 1949, they banned all golf courses saying it was the sport of millionaires. That lasted until the 1980s when the ban was lifted and the first new course was built in 1984 in Guangdong Province. As China became a world power and the people began having more spending money and leisure time, the country built lots of golf courses and many Chinese citizens, especially Chinese businesspeople, became passionate about golf. Playing golf became quite a status symbol. Then in 2004, a moratorium was placed on building golf courses in China. **The government said the ban was aimed at saving water, reducing pollution from fertilizers and pesticides, and "protecting the collective land of the peasants."** However, courses continued to be built and opened, mostly as part of China's real estate boom, and China now has well over 600 golf courses. **Over the past decade, no country in the world has built more golf courses than China.**

Many of the new courses were snuck in under the radar. Golf course builders ignored the ban and got creative, making sure the course was part of a large real estate development that helped disguise the golf course. **They avoided using the term golf in the name of the development** and often indicated on their plans that those large open spaces around which their new houses were being built were simply green space, an ecological reserve, or a special activities park.

At the present time, China is caught in a dilemma. Officially they don't approve of golf, but unofficially they love the sport and are very, very proud of the fact that several Chinese golfers are achieving some prominence in golf. Both on the women's tour and the men's tour, a few Chinese are moving up in the world rankings. **In fact, Shanshan Feng won the LPGA Championship in 2012 and is a multiple winner on the women's tour.** She is ranked as one of the top women golfers in the world. And China, which hosted the Beijing Summer Olympics in 2008, loves the Olympics and the exposure it gives their nation. They have a zeal for wanting to excel in all sports and now that golf has been added to the Olympics, they want to make sure they field a world-class golf team for each competition.

The Mission Hills 216 development in Shenzhen has been hugely successful, and despite the official ban on golf in the country, **another Mission Hills complex has been built in Haikou on Hainan Island,** which is located off the southeastern coast of China. Hainan has volcanic mountains, beautiful beaches, and is the only tropical island in China. Besides ten golf courses, Mission Hills Haikou has world-class resort hotels, elite restaurants, high-end shopping – and, get this, **168 natural hot and cold mineral spring pools.** Sounds to me like a great place to spend some time.

(Note – This chapter was first published in the author's book *Golfing – A View Through the Golf Hole.*)

Chinese Term

Wonton

A wonton is a tasty Chinese dumpling served boiled in a soup or sometimes fried as an appetizer. A popular filling in Hong Kong-style wontons is a mixture of ground minced pork, diced shrimp, green onions, garlic, and salt. When boiled, the thin wrapper becomes translucent. When fried, it becomes somewhat crispy and light brown.

Wonton soup is a hugely popular midday meal. Served up at sidewalk stands or small restaurants all over Hong Kong, you often need to come early for lunch or be prepared to queue up as you wait your turn. Then as you share a small table out on the street or inside the cramped eatery, be aware that napkins are not always provided. **So, bring your own tissue and then don't be afraid to eat as the locals do** – to slurp away as you polish off your soup with a Chinese porcelain soup spoon and some chopsticks. That's the way it's done.

And, as with hot dogs and so many other foods, there's a world record for eating wontons. **Consuming 390 in eight minutes** is the number to beat if you want to enter the record books.

Feng Shui

Situated on a mountainside overlooking a picturesque bay on the back side of Hong Kong Island is a beautiful high-rise building called **The Repulse Bay.** Containing residential units and a commercial arcade, The Repulse Bay looks pretty normal – except for one thing. **It has a huge hole right through the middle of it.** The hole is called **the dragon gate** and it was placed there because the developer of the building followed the advice of a feng shui master as the architects were designing the building. The hole gives the building excellent feng shui characteristics, **allowing the dragons that live in the hills behind the building to have unobstructed passage to the sea so they can quench their thirst and bathe.**

The Walt Disney Company consulted feng shui experts when it was designing **Hong Kong's Disneyland.** At the recommendation of the feng shui people, **the angle of the main entrance was shifted 12 degrees** to help ensure maximum prosperity for the theme park. Additionally, the pathway from the train station to the entry gate was modified from the original plan to prevent **qi, which is positive feng shui energy,** from slipping out of the gate and into the sea. (Qi is sometimes spelled chi or chee in English.)

When Hong Kong's last governor, **Chris Patten,** was replaced on July 1, 1997 by Hong Kong's first chief executive, **Tung Chee Hwa,** Governor Patten expected the new head of Hong Kong's government to move into Government House where Governor Patten had been living and working. But Tung Chee Hwa wouldn't do so.

He felt that Government House had poor feng shui because the nearby Bank of China building's sharp edges and corners reflected bad energy onto it. The new chief executive wasn't comfortable residing and working where bad feng shui might have a negative impact on his administration, so he never occupied Government House during the time of his service.

The Hong Kong government has paid out a number of **feng shui compensation payments** in recent years to some of its citizens. Why? **People living along a new express rail line running between Hong Kong and Guangzhou in mainland China claimed that the location of the line damaged their qi.** As a result, they had to hire feng shui masters to perform cleansing rituals along the rail line to reestablish the good feng shui. The government made the payments because of a law that says that anyone whose property is affected by a public construction project is entitled to compensation from the government (within certain restrictions) for any damage to their qi.

When Hong Kong's **Nina Wang** died of cancer in 2007, her fortune was estimated at HK$20.2 billion (US$2.6 billion), making her the wealthiest woman in Asia. So, guess who she willed the entire estate to? **You're right – to her beloved feng shui master, Tony Chan.** However, the authenticity of the will giving Mr. Chan all of the money was contested by Nina's family – and the feng shui master eventually lost a battle in court and ended up receiving nothing. Despite the court's ruling, many in Hong Kong feel that the will was valid and that Nina's intent was to give everything to Tony Chan because he had been so influential in helping her amass her wealth.

As a new office building on Hong Kong Island was nearing completion, a portion of the building's workforce refused to enter the main lobby to finish the job because they felt the lobby had bad feng shui. **The problem?** A huge mirror had been hung on the wall directly across from the entry door in a way that reflected everything coming into the building. **That violated the feng shui principle that a mirror should not be placed directly across from a front door because it will block energy flow and send positive qi right back out the building.** So, the building owners hired a feng shui master to help them move the mirror to a side wall and reorient the layout of the lobby. Once those things were done, the workers were happy to enter the building and finish their work.

What is Feng Shui?

Stemming from the ancient Chinese respect for the environment, feng shui is a philosophical system largely linked to Taoism that seeks to harmonize everyone and everything with their surroundings. **Literally translated as wind and water,** feng (wind) and shui (water) is pronounced fùng séui in Cantonese. A key element of feng shui is the belief in the existence of invisible forces that bind humanity, the earth, and the universe together. **These forces are known as qi.** Qi can rise over time as a result of the good use of feng shui, or diminish when feng shui is interrupted or the principles of feng shui are ignored.

A primary goal of feng shui is to take advantage of qi by appropriately siting buildings, homes, and other physical elements so they align with the energy of the earth. **When feng shui principles are followed so that objects and buildings are positioned in harmony with nature, qi flows into your life and honor, prosperity, blessings, and good fortune come to a person.** Since the principles of feng shui are extensive and can be somewhat complicated, experts in feng shui called **feng shui masters** are relied on to provide specific guidance as decisions are made.

Hong Kong and Feng Shui

In Hong Kong, feng shui is taken seriously, being perhaps the most important traditional Chinese concept embraced there. In terms of feng shui, Hong Kong's geographic setting is ideal. With mountains behind and water in front (water is strongly associated with wealth in feng shui), Hong Kong is naturally situated to take advantage of positive feng shui. Legend has it that Hong Kong's mountains are home to dragons that are said to bear positive and powerful energy. **Many Chinese believe that Hong Kong's positive natural feng shui has been a major contributing factor in the city's growth and prosperity over the years.**

Particularly when it comes to real estate, feng shui is important to the people of Hong Kong, as shown in the following excerpt from the *Amusing Planet* web magazine in March 2016:

"In Hong Kong, a city with one of the most beautiful skylines anywhere, **the plan and design of a building is determined as much by feng shui masters as by architects and engineers.** This ancient Chinese philosophy of positioning objects and buildings in harmony with nature to bring about good fortune, is deeply rooted in Hong Kong's culture. **Everything from the orientation of a building, the shape of the building, the position of the entrance, and the position of the furniture are believed to influence the prosperity of a business or homeowner.** Because of this belief, feng shui practitioners are consulted on almost every new home purchase and office floor plan – and even enormous architectural and engineering projects around this island nation are dictated to a large degree by feng shui."

Feng shui plays an active role in other aspects of a Hong Kong person's life, not just in real estate. Hong Kong's many feng shui masters are kept busy providing advice on a number of topics important to the Chinese, such as the following:

- **Selecting Auspicious Dates** – Feng shui masters are often consulted on the best and most auspicious dates for such things as holding weddings, scheduling store grand openings, making major purchases, moving into a new house, going on a trip, and having a child. Chinese believe that important events like these should take place when as many feng shui variables as possible are aligned in your favor.

- **Choosing Grave Sites** – The location and orientation of graves is a critical decision in the Chinese culture. Feng shui masters are looked at to provide expert advice on this subject. Ideal grave sites are located on hillsides that offer panoramic views to the deceased. To keep noxious winds from disturbing the qi, horseshoe-shaped walls and fences often surround the grave on three sides. All of this helps ensure a peaceful rest for the departed and enables them to more readily steer wealth and longevity to their heirs.

- **Naming Children** – In order to help ensure a long life with extra amounts of good fortune, feng shui masters are often asked to provide the names for newborn babies. Chinese names normally carry certain meanings and hopes from the parents, and wise parents are happy to pay a feng shui master to come up with a good name. In the words of Feng Shui Master Chan, who has practiced feng shui in Hong Kong for over 23 years:

  "A person's name is like a brand. Choosing an auspicious Chinese name is a very personal thing. **If the name is not done accurately, it does not sound good and it makes it difficult for the child to have a smooth journey in life.**"

- **Placing Fish Tanks in Restaurants** – Feng shui can also influence the design and layout of restaurants. When you go out to eat in Hong Kong, you'll often see a large fish tank near the entrance of the eating establishment because water improves feng shui and fish are believed to deflect evil. One reason it is believed fish can do this so well is because they are very observant – because their eyes are always open.

- **Laying Out Rooms in a House** – Feng shui provides guidance for laying out the rooms in a house, including the bedrooms. For bedrooms, feng shui principles say that:
  o The **bed** should ideally be placed diagonally opposite the bedroom door, with the head of the bed against something solid, like a wall.

- o The **mattress** should be new rather than used. Old mattresses may have accumulated negative energy from previous owners.
- o Bedroom and bathroom **mirrors** should not be placed directly facing the bed because mirrors facing the bed deplete your personal energy.
- o The best **artwork** for a bedroom is peaceful and calm. Aggressive artwork negates the feng shui energy that is needed to restore your body's health as you sleep.

Bedrooms should be passive spaces, not active ones like the kitchen or the home office. The bedroom's environment should promote the harmonious flow of nourishing energy that makes you want to relax rather than get things done. Good bedroom feng shui contributes to positive qi, **which leads to better sleep, improved personal relationships, and a flow of good fortune (think money) into your life.**

What Do You Think?

So, what do you think? Is feng shui just superstition, or is there something to it? Can feng shui actually generate more qi in your life? A lot of people in Hong Kong firmly believe in it, including many of the sophisticated and educated, **feeling that good feng shui can ward off bad luck and attract prosperity** – as new homes are purchased, offices are laid out, and architectural and engineering projects are undertaken. In fact, it is so important in Hong Kong that many engineers, architects, developers, real estate agents, and interior designers take feng shui courses as part of their training and certification in order to practice their professions in Hong Kong.

Personally, I find feng shui to be a fascinating subject, **and although I don't quite buy the dragon part of it,** some of the principles are quite rational and a lot of it seems to make good sense to me. While in Hong Kong, you might enjoy learning more about feng shui. Many books and classes are available and **there is even a popular Hong Kong feng shui city tour.** Sponsored by the Hong Kong Tourist Bureau, this interesting and informative tour costs HK$460 (US$60) and takes about three-and-a-half hours.

Chinese Term

Amah

An amah is a domestic servant who typically acts as both a maid and a nanny in a household in Hong Kong. Traditionally a Chinese person, **that role has now been filled primarily by foreign women who are referred to as domestic helpers.** At the present time, there are approximately **370,000** foreign domestic helpers in Hong Kong. Forty-eight percent of them come from the Philippines, forty-nine percent are from Indonesia, and two percent come from Thailand.

Because of this large group of workers in Hong Kong, the government has seen fit to draw up **rules and regulations** concerning their pay, job description, and employment conditions. Here are a few of the regulations:

- The domestic helper must work and live in the employer's place of residence and must be provided with suitable living accommodations and with reasonable privacy.
- A two-year standard contract is required between the employer and the employee.
- The domestic helper must be paid a monthly salary no less than the minimum wage set by the government.
- Free medical treatment must be provided.
- One rest day per week is required along with vacation time and holiday time.

With domestic helpers making up approximately 5% of the population, they are a large and visible part of Hong Kong, especially because they love to congregate outdoors on their days off. Look for hundreds of them nearly every day of the week at the World-Wide House in Central and Victoria Park in Causeway Bay where they gather to picnic and visit.

What Kind of Asian?

As I was nearing the finish of my college schooling, I was invited by an automobile company in Michigan to visit their headquarters in Dearborn to discuss possible employment with them. During an interview with one of the managers in the finance department, he noticed on my resume that I had lived in Hong Kong and that I spoke Chinese. **He excitedly said that there was a department head in his office from China, and he wanted us to get acquainted with each other and speak Chinese to each other.** The manager picked up his phone, dialed an extension, and invited the person on the other end of the line to come to his office. Soon, a nice-looking Asian man entered the office and was introduced to me as Jim. **Well, it turned out that the man was Jim Kobayashi, a native of Japan, and that he had never been to China and certainly could not speak Chinese.** Jim and I ended up becoming good friends during our time of employment together and often laughed about the mistake the manager made in mixing up China and Japan.

Have you ever done something like that? It's pretty easy to do. **To many westerners, all Asians seem to be alike.** Even after having lived in Hong Kong on two different occasions, I still am not that successful in knowing by sight which countries the Asians I meet are from. We don't always correctly recognize and differentiate between the people, the customs, the food, and the cultures of China, Japan, Korea, and other Asian nations.

Is it important to do so? I think it is. And it certainly is important to the people of Asia. **They have great national pride and don't appreciate it when we make mistakes in this regard.** Perhaps sometimes the mistakes can be comical and seem to be not very important, but at other times the mistakes we make can be quite hurtful and even rude – and they can make us appear foolish.

A few years ago, a major motion picture was released in the United States called *Memoirs of a Geisha.* The film generated great controversy. China banned it and many people in Japan refused to see it. Why? **A geisha is a traditional Japanese entertainer.** Geishas represent an impeccable and highly refined form of **Japanese** art. Geishas have no connection to China. **But all three of the main geishas in** *Memoirs of a Geisha* **were portrayed by Chinese actresses.** (Actually, two were Chinese and one was an ethnic Chinese from Malaysia.) To the movie moguls in Hollywood, the ethnicity of the actresses wasn't important so long as they were Asian and could act, but to the Asian viewing public, the miscasting was a huge mistake.

Let's take a look at some of the things that help us distinguish one Asian country and its people and customs from the others. For simplicity's sake in this chapter, let's just focus on two countries, China and Japan, as we make the comparisons.

- **Names** – Almost all Chinese surnames are just **one syllable**. Almost all Japanese surnames are made up of **three or more syllables**. Wong, Chan, Lee, and Fong are all Chinese surnames. Yamaguchi, Matsumori, Tanaka, and Yamamoto are Japanese surnames. (And notice how often a Japanese surname ends in an a, i, or o.

- **Food** – While it is true that China and Japan share some ingredients and cooking methods, **their cuisines are distinctly different.** Both China and Japan have rice as their main food staple – and both eat lots of noodles. Japanese food tends to have a more subtle flavor. Chinese, on the other hand, has stronger flavors and relies more heavily on stir frying as a cooking method. Traditional Japanese foods include tempura, sushi, teriyaki, miso soup, sukiyaki, and sashimi. Egg drop soup, beef with broccoli, kung pao chicken, Peking duck, and honey walnut shrimp are traditional Chinese dishes. **Both cultures use chopsticks,** but Chinese chopsticks are heavier, longer, blunt, and typically reusable while Japanese chopsticks tend to be shorter, thinner, pointy, and they are often used just once before being discarded.

CHINESE CHEONGSAM   JAPANESE KIMONO

- **Clothing** – Many women in China wear **cheongsams**. The typical cheongsams are beautiful body-hugging full-length dresses, often with a long slit down the side of one of the legs. In the Chinese language, cheongsam means long dress. **Kimonos**, on the other hand, are Japanese. Traditional kimonos are loose fitting T-shaped, full-length garments with wide sleeves. A wide sash called an obi is wrapped around the waist to secure the dress. Both cheongsams and kimonos are absolutely gorgeous – but don't mix them up if you want to keep your Chinese and Japanese friends happy.
- **Language** – Although both the Chinese and Japanese languages sound very foreign and perhaps quite similar to

each other to the western ear, they are very different languages. Chinese is a tonal language whereas Japanese is not. Although Japanese has no genetic relationship with Chinese, it does make use of some Chinese characters in its writing system. **The fact that someone speaks Chinese does not mean they can speak and understand Japanese, and vice versa.**

- **New Year** – **The Chinese celebrate Chinese New Year. The Japanese do not.** After all, it is called **Chinese New Year** for a reason. So, don't call your Japanese friends and wish them kung hei fat choi and invite them out to dinner at a Chinese restaurant in late January or early February to celebrate Chinese New Year. But do invite your Japanese acquaintances to join your New Year's Eve party on December 31. They would be honored to be included.
- **What is Shared?** – What is shared among China and Japan? In general terms, some physical features, some foods, some cultural mannerisms, some writing, some martial arts, and some religious philosophies are shared.

In my mind, both China and Japan are wonderful countries with tremendous heritages and fascinating cultures, as are Korea, Vietnam, Cambodia, Taiwan, and others. Neither China nor Japan is better than the other – **but they are quite different from each other** – and we need to remember that factor and think twice before we stick our foot in our mouth when interacting with Asian people.

Oh, and one more example to show how good the west is at getting things mixed up and stepping on Asian toes. My favorite book about China is *The Good Earth* by **Pearl S. Buck.** It is a marvelous account of how life was lived in rural China prior to World War I. Published in 1931, Ms. Buck won both a Pulitzer Prize and a Nobel Prize for the book. In 1937, it came out as a Hollywood movie. There are six principal Chinese characters in the book *The Good Earth.*

And guess what? **Western Caucasian actors and actresses, not Chinese, were chosen to play every one of these six lead characters in the movie** – even though there were a number of good Chinese actors and actresses available in Hollywood at that time. How do you think the Chinese felt about that?

(Note – If you haven't read *The Good Earth*, I highly recommend it. Chapter 3 is especially interesting. It tells the touching story of O-lan giving birth to her first child on her own with no assistance from anyone else after she has toiled all morning in the fields alongside her husband, Wang Lung.)

Chinese Term

Junks

Junks are a type of Chinese sailing ship characterized by a flat wooden hull, uniquely shaped red sails with battens, and a high deck at the rear of the boat. (A batten is a thin strip of wood inserted into a sail to strengthen the sail and keep it flat.) **The ship on the cover of this book is a junk.** Junks – which are efficient, sturdy, and excellent for carrying cargo – have sailed the harbors, bays, and seas of Hong Kong for many years.

Benjamin Franklin was especially impressed with one feature of the Chinese junks he had heard about. This feature was that many junks had a series of compartments or holds built inside the hull to strengthen the ship and to slow flooding in case a portion of the hull was ruptured. In 1787, Franklin got involved in the design of vessels that carried mail between the U.S. and France and advised the designers of the ships to pattern the holds after those in Chinese junks. He said, **"...the holds should be divided into separate apartments, after the Chinese manner, and each of these apartments caulked tight so as to keep out water."**

If you are interested in taking a ride on a junk while in Hong Kong, there are several companies that offer tours. **One especially enjoyable excursion is aboard a beautiful authentic junk called the Duk Ling.** It provides 45-minute trips around Victoria Harbour for a fee. The Duk Ling picks up passengers at Tsim Sha Tsui's Pier 1 on the Kowloon side and at Central Pier 9 on the island side of the harbor.

Two other types of Chinese boats seen in the harbors of Hong Kong are **walla-wallas** and **sampans**. Both are smaller than junks. **Walla-wallas are motorboats that operate around the harbors as water taxis.** They are named for the pulsating puttering sound the engines make. **Sampans are small flat-bottomed boats used for a variety of purposes, including fishing.** Propelled by a single oar at the stern (or by an outboard motor in more modern versions), some sampans include a simple onboard shelter to protect against the elements.

The Rise and Fall of Hong Kong's Famous Neon Signs

I hope you have the opportunity of strolling along Hong Kong's crowded streets at night to view the dazzling neon signs that are so prevalent throughout the city. They are an integral part of Hong Kong's culture and have helped make Hong Kong such an interesting place to visit.

Although there are a number of places in Hong Kong where the viewing of neon signs is especially good, **perhaps my favorite place to do so is on Nathan Road in Tsim Sha Tsui.** I recommend this location because the Nathan Road shopping area has the dubious distinction of having **the highest light pollution measurement in all of Hong Kong** – and Hong Kong has one of the highest light pollution measurements of any city on earth.

Light pollution is defined as the presence of artificial light in a night environment, and because this is usually thought to be a negative thing, most places do their best to cut down on light pollution. But when the merchants in Tsim Sha Tsui heard that they were the brightest nighttime spot in all of Hong Kong and perhaps in all the world, **they celebrated, realizing that their amazing concentration of neon signs gave them a degree of notoriety that was really good for business.**

I would suggest you start your sign-viewing journey at the corner of Nathan Road and Salisbury Road by the Peninsula Hotel and walk up Nathan Road (i.e. go north in the direction away from the harbor). Nathan Road is one of Hong Kong's most fascinating and bustling streets. You will see hundreds of neon signs in all shapes, sizes, and colors on the fronts, sides, and tops of the buildings. **And you will notice one of Hong Kong's distinctive visual fingerprints – the neon signs that cantilever out over the streets, often overlapping each other.** As you walk, besides noticing the signs on Nathan Road itself, pay attention to the densely packed neon signs on the narrow side streets along the way (like on Peking Road and Humphreys Avenue). For blocks and blocks, you will notice a dazzling array of hundreds of neon signs – on tailor shops, jewelry stores, electronic shops, nightclubs, hotels, souvenir shops, restaurants, clothing stores, pharmacies, and pawn shops.

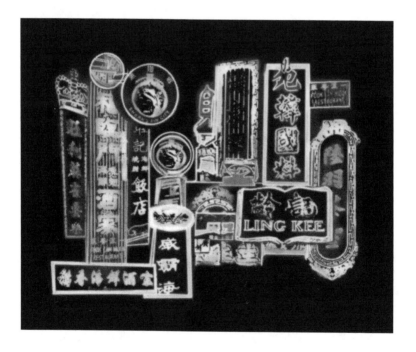

Then, part way up the street (after walking about eight to ten blocks), finish your sign-viewing outing by boarding one of the double-decker buses heading further up Nathan Road (#2 and #6 are good choices) to get a closer view of the many additional signs along the road, especially the ones hanging over the street. **I recommended that you sit on the top deck of the bus in the very front seat, if possible.** As the bus lurches and sways while making its way up the street, it will seem to barely fit under and around many of the signs. During the ride, imagine in your mind the special artistic skill and technical ability required to design, fabricate, and install each neon sign. **Notice especially the complexity of the Chinese characters and how each character has been carefully reproduced in neon tubing by the sign makers.** And consider the fact that many of the world's largest and most notable neon signs are found in Hong Kong – situated along its congested streets and located on the sides, faces, and tops of the huge buildings that line both sides of Hong Kong's beautiful harbor.

As is the case with many inventions, neon signs came about somewhat by accident. Here is a brief portion of that story, as told by Steven Johnson in his excellent book *How We Got to Now*:

"While neon is technically considered one of the "rare gases," it is actually ubiquitous in the earth's atmosphere, just in small quantities. **Each time you take a breath, you are inhaling a tiny amount of neon, mixed in with all the nitrogen and oxygen that saturate breathable air.** In the first years of the twentieth century, a French scientist named Georges Claude created a system for liquefying air, which enabled the production of large quantities of liquid nitrogen and oxygen. **Processing these elements at industrial scale created an intriguing waste product: neon.** With so much neon lying around, Claude decided to see if it was good for anything, and so in proper mad-scientist fashion, he isolated the gas and passed an electrical current through it. **Exposed to the charge, the gas glowed a vivid shade of red.**"

It wasn't long before Claude discovered that he could also make other gases such as argon, xenon, helium, and krypton, or combinations of these gases and other chemicals, glow to produce a variety of bright colors. He then set about to develop a system of placing these gases in sealed glass tubes and electrifying them. **He patented his efforts and called his invention neon lights.** (Calling them neon lights is a bit of a misnomer. Although neon is the predominant gas used, it is actually just one of several gases and chemicals found in neon lighting.)

As Claude began promoting his invention, neon signs started appearing in various places around the world, including Hong Kong. Most of the signs were simple window signs or small signs mounted flush on the fronts of stores. **But it wasn't long before Hong Kong's sign makers embraced the technology** and became known as some of the leading experts in the world in designing and installing innovative neon signs, **especially ones that were cantilevered out from buildings, extending past the sidewalks and out over the roads.**

Hong Kong merchants caught on quickly to the advantage of having this bright and highly visible signage and began working to outdo each other with bigger and more spectacular signs. Soon, the city's narrow streets were filled with neon signs, **creating stunning visual images that quickly became some of Hong Kong's most recognizable features.** Along with its fantastic food and incredible shopping bargains, Hong Kong became known for its amazing lights and a skyline that transformed its appearance as the day changed to night.

Hong Kong's neon signs date back to the 1920s. At first, just small one- or two-person shops were involved in making the signs. Because of the complexity of the neon tube shaping and the requirement of having to often hang the signs in tight and tricky locations, **each sign maker had to wear many hats – artist, designer, structural engineer, glass blower, electrician, sheet metal fabricator, painter, installer, and repair person.** Crafting a neon sign required an engineer's mind, an electrician's logic, and an artist's eye.

Over time, sign-making techniques improved, sign companies proliferated, and more sophisticated and showy neon signs sprouted up everywhere. **The industry grew quickly, with the 1960s through 1990s being the golden age of neon signs in Hong Kong.** Hong Kong became a city of vibrant, flashy, and captivating signs that became an ingrained part of Hong Kong's image. In many locations, entire façades of huge buildings were covered in neon, gaining world-wide notoriety and awards for the sponsors of the signs. (For instance, the Panasonic neon sign on Nathan Road, a world record when it was erected in the 1970s, covered the entire width and height of the high-rise building it was on, even extending well above the structure's roof line.)

Then the LED light came along. Although LED (Light-Emitting Diode) technology had been around for a while, it wasn't until the early 2000s that it advanced to the point where it became practical to use LED lights for outdoor signs. **With the emergence of LED, it became harder to justify the extra effort and cost that**

neon signs required, especially since LED lights could be arrayed and configured to simulate and approximate the look of neon signs. Today, LED is the preferred lighting method for outdoor advertising in Hong Kong and elsewhere, being cheaper to produce, faster to make, less expensive to operate, more versatile in its design, and much longer-lasting than neon signs.

As a result, Hong Kong's neon sign-making industry is now in danger of disappearing, as are the once highly valued neon sign makers. Today, only a handful of those artists remain and most of them are getting along in years. Fewer neon signs are being made and when an existing neon sign needs repairing, it is often taken down and replaced with a new LED one.

Although the new LED signs look great, I will always have a fondness for the neon ones. For me, LED will never quite replace the unique look and special feel of Hong Kong's old neon signs. While Hong Kong is still known for its dazzling signs and brilliant lights, now only a portion of Hong Kong's dazzle comes from actual neon signs.

Alas, times are changing in Hong Kong as they are everywhere. And while I am in favor of innovation and progress, I remain a bit old-fashioned. I still think the greatest car ever made was the 1957 Thunderbird with the porthole window, that newspapers are meant to be in paper form and delivered to your door, that you should dress up when attending the symphony, and that vinyl records are superior to CDs. What do you think?

Chinese Term

Yin and Yang

For thousands of years, the Chinese have observed that nature involves the interplay of opposites – **light and dark, male and female, heat and cold.** Their observations led them to develop a philosophy of thought that says that everything has its opposite and that opposites are complementary and necessary in the proper operation of the universe. **Harmony is achieved when the forces of nature are in balance.**

They call the two opposite forces **yin and yang** and Chinese people, particularly the Taoists, view the world, including human beings in the world, in terms of how yin and yang work together. This relationship is illustrated using the black and white symbol shown on the next page. **The black portion is yin – which represents dark, negative, feminine, and passive. The white portion is yang – which is bright, positive, masculine, and active.** The two forces are interdependent and complementary, flowing back and forth, into and away from each other, ebbing and flowing to maintain the natural balance of nature.

Picture, for instance, a calm pool of water. Dropping a stone in the water will simultaneously raise waves and lower troughs. This pattern of high and low will radiate outward until the movements begin to dissipate – and then they disappear. The pool of water will return to being calm once again. **Such is nature. Such is yin and yang.** Ebb and flow. In and out. Up and down. Active and passive. Good and evil. Male and female. Light and dark. Hard and soft. Turmoil and harmony. **Yin and yang.**

The Chinese who follow this school of thinking believe that **the interaction of yin and yang is a constant part of life.** Wise persons search to understand these two forces and to regulate their lives in accordance with them so as to achieve proper balance and harmony.

(Note – There is an old Hollywood movie from the early 1970s about yin and yang. Filmed in Hong Kong and starring Jeff Bridges, it is called *The Yin and the Yang of Mr. Go.* It is an action movie about how the Chinese principle of yin and yang has the power to turn an evil villain into a heroic good guy.)

Of Coffin Homes and Mansions

I am writing this chapter while sitting at my desk in my home office. It is a comfortably sized office that measures 12 feet wide by 11 feet deep. The total floor area of my office is 132 square feet.

At the present time in Hong Kong, **there are some 200,000 people living in tiny homes called coffin homes (also known as cage homes and shoe box homes)** that measure less than the size of my office. In fact, some are so small that three or four of these coffin homes could fit into the space taken up by my office. Here are some examples:

- There is a 3-foot by 6-foot space in the Hung Hom area that is occupied by an elderly male. Crammed into this **18-square-foot coffin home** are his possessions – a sleeping bag, small TV, cooking top, and electric fan. He has a number of neighbors on the same floor of this old building who live in similar circumstances.

- A woman with an 8-year-old daughter and a 6-year-old son lives in a 110-square-foot apartment in Kowloon. **The total living space for these three people is less than what I have in my office.** Included in this tight living space are a small sink and a rickety toilet. A hose can be attached to the faucet in the sink so that a shower can be taken while standing over the toilet.

- A 300-square-foot flat in Kennedy Town has been **illegally subdivided to accommodate 15 inhabitants.** Each one of these 15 coffin homes has a plywood bunk propped up on boxes to serve as a bed and a rickety sliding panel across the front to provide some privacy. Located down the hall, a small kitchen, shower, and toilet are available for the tenants to share.
- A retired janitor lives in a **50-square-foot place** in the Yau Tsim Mong district. He has been on a waiting list for government housing for several years.

On the other end of the spectrum, a luxurious mansion on Victoria Peak was recently listed for sale at US$446 million (HK$3.5 billion). Although not extremely large (it measures less than 8,000 square feet) it is a magnificent property with a stunning outdoor pool and terrific views. When it sells, probably at or above the listing price, **it will go on record as the most expensive piece of residential real estate ever sold in Hong Kong** – and when valued on a square foot basis, it will perhaps be the most expensive ever in the world. The buyer will probably be someone from mainland China or a wealthy

Hong Kong business person. This mansion is not an isolated case. **During a recent calendar year, there were a number of residential homes sales in Hong Kong in excess of US$100 million each.** Beginning in 1949, soon after the end of World War II, Hong Kong faced the tremendous task of trying to provide proper and affordable housing for its residents. **During that year alone, more than 200,000 refugees swarmed across the border to live in Hong Kong.** They occupied anything and everything that provided even the slightest bit of shelter – hillside tin and cardboard shanties, rooftop huts, and even tiny stairwells. That in-migration movement continued for a number of years, making the providing of adequate housing one of the colony's most difficult challenges. **From 1945 to 1951, the population of Hong Kong grew from 600,000 to 2.1 million.**

Then, on Christmas day 1953, a huge fire swept through the Shek Kip Mei area of Kowloon **that left 53,000 people homeless and in desperate need of shelter.** The Hong Kong government's response to that tragedy attracted worldwide attention as it instituted an emergency housing program that put in motion a plan to create **"resettlement estates"** throughout the colony. Those huge resettlement estates, and Hong Kong's famous **"new towns"** in more recent years, have become the prototype for housing authorities around the world. Today, of Hong Kong's 7.5 million people, more than half live in rental and for sale housing that has been provided by the government under its housing authority department.

Despite these efforts over the years, Hong Kong is still in a housing crisis. **There are just too many people and there is not enough developable land to satisfactorily house everyone.** The Hong Kong Housing Authority stated in a recent annual report:

"The government has flagged housing as a top priority in its planning. **The urgent plan is to design and build 280,000 flats in Hong Kong during the next ten years – 200,000 for rent and 80,000 for sale – along with 180,000 private homes.** To meet this challenge, the Housing Authority is bringing all of its experience, means, and resources to bear. Its rich local design and planning abilities, its advanced technology, its efficient and sustainable construction techniques and management strategies, and its dedicated and committed personnel – all these are combining to rise to the challenge of increasing supply, in the service of a better Hong Kong for the future."

This task is a daunting one. Some of the specific initiatives that are part of their long-term plan include:

- **Reclaiming Land – Along with the Dutch, Hong Kong is an expert in land reclamation.** Although visitors don't always realize it, most of the harbor-front buildings you see on Hong Kong Island sit on land that has been created where there once was sea. The same is true of the Kowloon Peninsula. The time it now takes for the Star Ferry to travel from Kowloon to the island is a lot less than when I first rode the Star Ferry in 1966. **The harbor is now much narrower and smaller because of all the reclaimed land.** Other areas of Hong Kong, especially in the New Territories, have huge new towns that have been built on land that previously was sea or other bodies of water. The new airport sits on reclaimed land created from two former islands and the new third runway being built parallel to the current two runways will be on reclaimed land. Even a large portion of Hong Kong Disneyland sits on reclaimed land. Many projects to reclaim additional land for housing and other development are underway.

- **Building Artificial Islands** – Being done specifically to create more land for housing, **Hong Kong is in the process of creating several new large artificial islands in the sea.** Although extremely costly and requiring many years to complete, these new islands will be a major help in alleviating Hong Kong's housing problems. An example of this effort is a massive project east of Lantau Island where two artificial islands are being planned that would house an additional 1.1 million people.

- **Developing on Mountainsides** – One of the challenges of Hong Kong's geography is that **so much of Hong Kong's land is mountainous.** A number of areas of formerly uninhabitable mountain terrain have already been leveled and developed into housing and more areas are going through this same process in order to create places for large new high-rise developments.

- **Using Innovative Housing Ideas** – Although somewhat extreme in some cases, with the help of experts from around the world, **Hong Kong is looking at new and innovative ideas to house its population.** Several ultra-high-density housing ideas being considered include:

o **Capsules** – Designed as living spaces for one or two persons, these capsules or pods **would typically be prefabricated,** often out of plastic, and come furnished with a TV, air conditioning, tables, beds, mattresses, and lighting fixtures. They would be placed side by side and on top of one another in ways that would provide comfortable and clean housing for quite a few people.

o **Drain Pipes** – Architects have proposed using **huge concrete drain pipes** for housing. Two long repurposed drainpipes would be placed end to end to create a small, but livable home that would include a kitchenette, bathroom, shower, eating area, and convertible bed. The homes would be designed so they could be stacked up to five high.

o **Shipping Containers** – Also being done elsewhere in the world, shipping containers turned into housing units is not only possible, **but is even somewhat trendy.** Stacked and arranged in an attractive manner, the containers would have windows and some would even have balconies. One of the nice aspects of this proposal, is that Hong Kong is one of the world's leading container ports, so a supply of used shipping containers is readily available.

Hong Kong has a history of being able to overcome difficult and challenging situations. It is a unique and vibrant city with a highly intelligent populace who have an amazing ability to solve problems and achieve great things. **Although I'm not sure the huge disparity between coffin homes and luxurious mansions will ever disappear,** I am confident that they will make great progress in the coming years in conquering the housing crisis. **If anyone can pull it off, Hong Kong can.** I'll be eagerly watching to see how they do it.

Chinese Term

MSG

It's quite common to see a sign in the window of a Chinese restaurant that says, **"No MSG."** Short for **monosodium glutamate**, MSG is an additive used in the food industry as a flavor enhancer, especially in some Chinese cooking. Although not really a Chinese term, I thought I'd write about MSG because it is so often associated with Chinese food.

Why do Chinese restaurants boldly proclaim "No MSG"? In 1968 in the U.S., there were reports of serious reactions to the food served in some Chinese restaurants. The reactions included headaches, flushing, numbness around the mouth, sweating, and even chest pain. The problem got a lot of press and was widely publicized. **MSG was blamed for causing the problem.**

The U.S. Food and Drug Administration (FDA) undertook studies of Chinese food and MSG to see what might be happening. The research included double-blind trials in a number of different clinics and settings. The results? **There was no evidence that either Chinese food or MSG used as an additive in the food was the problem.** Something else about the food or the restaurant experience was causing the symptoms. The FDA gave MSG its **"generally recognized as safe" (GRAS) designation**, and that designation still exists for it today.

But the cat was out of the bag, so to speak. **The damage had already been done.** Consumers were convinced that MSG was harmful, especially the MSG used in Chinese restaurants. So, in the decades since then, Chinese restaurants, especially those in the U.S., have made it a point to not use MSG and to clearly tell their customers that they don't.

Even if MSG doesn't cause illness, **it does contain quite a bit of sodium** (about 12% in mass content compared to about 39% in regular table salt), so it probably is wise not to use too much of it anyway. But if you want to avoid monosodium glutamate completely, you'll need to be careful with lots of foods, not just Chinese food, **because MSG occurs naturally in tomatoes, cheese, and to a lesser degree, in yeast extracts, cornstarch, pectin, and caramel flavorings.**

Confucius Says...

It seems like sayings and proverbs attributed to Confucius and China are everywhere these days. They are used frequently by business leaders, educators, writers, and self-help speakers to encourage and motivate us in our quest for more wisdom and greater success. I've recently seen the following sayings in my travels around our community:

- **Local Library** – As I walked into our local library, I noticed the following saying prominently displayed in the entry foyer: "A book is like a garden carried in a pocket."
- **Car Dealership** – A car salesman we recently dealt with had the following framed saying hanging on the wall of his cubicle: "Fall down seven times. Get up eight."
- **School Room** – A classroom in a school I visited had the following written on the whiteboard: "Your teacher can open the door, but you must enter by yourself."
- **Football Locker Room** – Shown during a TV broadcast of a football game, the locker room of the home team had the following saying painted in bold letters on a wall: " Do not pray for an easy journey, pray for the strength to endure a difficult one."
- **Copy Shop** – Above the door of a copy shop in our area was the following saying: "A happy customer brings back many more."

All of the above sayings had the source of the saying written after it. **Each one indicated that it was either a "Confucius says," a "Chinese proverb," or a "Chinese saying."** China and Confucius received credit for all of them.

A proverb is a simple saying that expresses a truth based on common sense and experience. Whether we refer to them as proverbs, maxims, fortune cookie fortunes, truisms, idioms, or just wise sayings, **proverbs are small packages of truth reflecting the values and beliefs of a people.** And taken as a group, they represent a vast treasure of wisdom, culture, and guidance for us all.

China is given credit for being the originator of more proverbs and sayings than any other country on earth and the man Confucius,

known to his students and followers as Master Confucius, is the clear leader in China for coming up with them. Today, you can look up hundreds, if not thousands, of Confucius sayings in books and on the internet.

Confucius, who lived in China from 551 BC until 479 BC, was a prolific teacher, philosopher, and motivator. Although he did not personally write down his teachings, his students did the writing for him, compiling a number of books of his sayings after his death. **The best known of these is called *The Analects of Confucius*, which is a large collection of his wisdom and teachings.** In that book, his many sayings are usually preceded with the words, "The Master says...," hence our custom of writing "Confucius says..." when we quote him.

Confucius gets credit for a lot of sayings that are not really his. As an example, the one in the car dealership about falling down and getting back up is, according to several places on the internet, a Japanese proverb rather than a Confucius saying. **Who the original writer is of wise sayings and maxims is not always clear because there have been so many sages, writers, and philosophers over the years who have said and written so many similar things.**

For instance, we might ask who first came up with what we call **The Golden Rule.** Confucius appears to have been one of the earliest ones to teach this idea when he said in Chapter XV of *Analects,* **"What you do not wish for yourself, do not do to others,"** but similar maxims are found in some form in many religions and cultures. Here are a few of them:

- **Ancient India** – "Do not do to others what you know has hurt yourself." (*Tirukkural*, Chapter 32)
- **Ancient Rome** – "Treat your inferior as you would wish your superior to treat you." (Essay by Seneca the Younger)
- **Christianity** – "Therefore all things whatsoever ye would that men should do to you, do ye even so to them." (Jesus Christ's Sermon on the Mount, *Matthew 7:12*)
- **Ancient Greece** – "Do not do to others that which angers you when they do it to you." (Isocrates in the *Nicocles Discourse*)
- **Ancient Persia** – "That nature alone is good which refrains from doing to another whatsoever is not good for itself." (*Pahlavi Texts*)
- **Islam** – "That which you want for yourself, seek for mankind." (*Conversations with Muhammad*)

While we are not always able to determine who said something first, **Confucius certainly is regarded as the most prolific of all of the producers of sayings** (along with the Hallmark card people). His proverbs seem to get the majority of the press today and he is the recognized leader in not only the number, but also the wide scope of his sayings – as they cover a large range of subjects including knowledge, happiness, wisdom, virtue, prosperity, love, fortune, politics, relationships, character, etc.

If we were to summarize **the focus of the sayings of Confucius,** we might come up with something like the following list:

- **Live Authentically** – Live an authentic life and be honest in your choices, no matter how immaterial they may seem.
- **Think Deeply** – In order to genuinely appreciate life, you must think deeply and use the total capacity of your mind.
- **Persevere** – Regardless of the size of the task ahead of you, if you start small and stay with it, good results will occur. Have faith in yourself and believe that everything you do matters.
- **Live a Moral Life** – Both individuals and their governments should strive to do what is moral and right.
- **Be Practical** – Infuse your life with ideas and goals that have immediate practical application. Be wary of teachings that sound good in theory but cannot be reasonably put into practice.
- **Have Correct Social Relationships** – Strive to make all relationships correct and proper.

The people of Hong Kong love Chinese proverbs and the sayings of Confucius, using them regularly in their dealings with each other. They are proud of their Chinese sayings **and take great delight in the fact that the western world uses them frequently** and that westerners see Chinese culture and Chinese sages, such as Confucius, as being so wise and important.

I also enjoy Confucian sayings and Chinese maxims and try to implement their teachings as I go through my life. **Here are some of my personal favorites:**

- "It does not matter how slowly you go so long as you do not stop."
- "I hear and I forget. I see and I remember. I do and I understand."
- "The superior man is modest in his speech, but exceeds in his actions."
- "When is the best time to plant a tree? A hundred years ago. When is the second-best time? Today."
- "The person who says it cannot be done should not interrupt the person doing it."
- "Learning is a treasure that will follow its owner everywhere."
- "They who know the truth are not equal to those who love it, and they who love it are not equal to those who delight in it."
- "When you have faults, do not fear to abandon them."
- "Everything has its beauty, but not everyone sees it."
- "Forget injuries, but never forget kindness."

Chinese Term

Simplified Characters

Simplified characters are easier and quicker to write than traditional Chinese characters. **They require fewer strokes of the pen or brush.** As shown in the example below, the traditional Chinese character for the word horse requires ten strokes to make. The new simplified character can be made with just three strokes.

Developed in the People's Republic of China beginning in 1949, simplified characters were introduced to promote literacy. Today, the simplified script is used in China and Singapore, **but it has never been officially adopted in Hong Kong, Taiwan, and Macau.**

Character for Horse

Traditional (10 strokes)   Simplified (3 strokes)

Let's Relax in Macau

Hong Kong has been described as a city with never-ending action, excitement, movement, jostling, scurrying, and scrambling. So, in 1968, when I needed a diversion and wanted to get away from the hustle and bustle of Hong Kong, I went with friends to Macau. Today, that still is what many Hong Kong people do. **When they need a break, they head for Macau.**

Like Hong Kong, Macau is now a Special Administrative Region (SAR) of China. Established in 1557 by Portugal, it was Europe's first colony in Asia. In 1999, China brought it back into its fold as they did with Hong Kong in 1997. With a population of nearly 700,000, Macau is a fascinating blend of ethnicities, cultures, customs, foods, and languages. Although the present population is approximately 90% Chinese, there are still a number of true Macanese living there **(the Macanese are the native-born people with mixed Portuguese ancestry).** Many from countries such as the Philippines, Vietnam, Malaysia, and Indonesia also reside and work there.

Getting from Hong Kong to Macau is quite easy. A fast hydrofoil jet boat can take you there in less than an hour. And a new 34-mile bridge from Hong Kong to Macau that was completed in 2018 allows cars, buses, and trucks from Hong Kong to travel there as well. **The bridge and tunnel system, called the Hong Kong-Zhuhai-Macau Bridge, has the distinction of being the longest sea crossing on earth.** At a cost of US$18.8 billion, it is quite an engineering and construction marvel. Macau is also serviced by an international airport.

There are many things in Macau that draw millions of visitors each year to this former Portuguese colony, such as:

- **The Pace** – Macau is still a fast-paced and vibrant city, but compared to Hong Kong it moves a bit slower. Although crowded with motorcycles, buses, taxis, cars, and people, **it tends to be a more relaxed city** – of course, compared to Hong Kong, just about anywhere in the world is a more relaxed place.

- **Cuisine** – With both Cantonese and Portuguese influences,

the food in Macau is excellent and plentiful – and a bit different from Hong Kong's cuisine. When Hong Kong people visit Macau, they descend on its restaurants with great gusto, hoping to try something a bit new and different from what they are used to. And Macau doesn't disappoint, being legendary for the diversity of its cuisine. You may want to choose to dine at *A Lorcha, the Flamingo Restaurant, or the Military Club* for a taste of authentic Macanese dishes such as braised duck with tomatoes, Macanese-style crab, African chicken, and partridge pie. And for a delicious treat when out on the street, **try some Portuguese egg tarts.** I like them best when they have just come out of the oven and are still warm.

- **Old Sights** – The city is full of sights from Macau's earlier days. Don't miss the dramatic free-standing façade of the old 16th century **São Paulo Church**, the impressive grand staircase that descends from the church, Senado Square, the Guia Mount Fortress, and the historic A-Ma Temple.

- **Two Noteworthy Annual Events** – Each year, Macau hosts two especially noteworthy events:
  - **The international fireworks competition** held in September is as good as it gets. Bringing together **the best fireworks displays from twelve different nations,** the contest is held over six nights. Put to music, each country's fireworks presentation is set off from barges in the harbor, with each production lasting about 15 minutes. The winning trophy is one of the most coveted international awards in the pyrotechnics industry.
  - **Macau's annual Grand Prix race weekend** draws the best racers from around the world. Held in November, it is the only street circuit racing event in the world involving both cars and motorcycles. (They compete at separate times, of course.) **The highlight of the race weekend is the exciting Macau Formula Three Grand Prix Race.**

- **Gambling** – Live and online gambling is outlawed in both mainland China and Hong Kong – but not in Macau. Since 2007, Macau has held the distinction of **surpassing even Las Vegas** in gross gambling revenue. Many of Macau's casinos are virtual duplicates of ones in Las Vegas, having been built by the same companies. Such Las Vegas-type attractions as a large outdoor fountain set to music and lights, a ½-scale Eiffel Tower, and a Venetian canal are also found in Macau.

- **Bungee Jump** – And, if you have the time and courage (and the funds), you might try out one more interesting activity in Macau. The Macau Tower bungee jump is 764 feet high, making this jump off the edge of the beautiful tower next to the harbor **the second highest commercial bungee jump in the world.**

As you plan your trip to Hong Kong, taking an extra day or two to travel to Macau will be well worth your while. It is a scenic, interesting, and relaxing place to visit – at least it is relaxing compared to Hong Kong – and it's something I think you'll be glad you did.

Chinese Term

Saving Face

A young businessman interrupts his Hong Kong boss's presentation in a company planning meeting and says, "Mr. Wong, I think that there is a better way to do what you are talking about." Mr. Wong is caught off guard and is embarrassed. **He has lost face among his employees.**

President Hu Jin Tao, the president of China, visits the U.S. in 2006, but his visit is designated by the U.S. government as merely an "official visit" instead of a "state visit." (A state visit is the highest form of diplomatic contact that can be granted a foreign dignitary.) Instead of a black-tie formal state dinner at the White House with the U.S. president, President Hu only has a luncheon with the president and other U.S. political leaders. Then, to add insult to injury, as President Hu and his delegation are welcomed, the announcer announces that the U.S. band will play the national anthem of the Republic of China. **But Hu Jin Tao is the president of the People's Republic of China.** The Republic of China is Taiwan. **President Hu, as well as the 1.4 billion citizens of China, have lost face.**

A Chinese couple in Hong Kong works hard to provide a quality education for their daughter. The result is that the girl is accepted into a prestigious foreign university. **The parents have gained face among their family and peers.**

Face is a person's prestige, honor, and reputation. While we westerners are also aware of face and consider it to be important in our society, the Chinese step it up several notches. **In China, face is a person's most valued possession.** Because face is the product of human interactions, **tact and diplomacy in dealing with the Chinese**

are indispensable in our relations with them and we would be wise to do all we can to help our Chinese associates **save face** as we interact with them.

By the way, **in 2011 President Hu was able to regain his lost face.** The U.S. invited him back, this time for a formal **state visit** that included all the ceremonies and honors typically accorded an important head of state, including a black-tie dinner at the White House.

144 Noisy Tiles

Mother to disobedient child: "Don't make me use my mahjong voice."

Mahjong is said to be the noisiest parlor game in the world. But it's not just the 144 tiles clattering on the mahjong table that cause the ruckus. It is also the constant chatter and socializing that take place among the participants in the game, often at quite a high decibel level, that help give it this distinction. The whole occasion surrounding a game of mahjong makes for a loud, sociable, exciting, and competitive event – especially when the game is taking place in Hong Kong.

Originating in China many centuries ago, mahjong initially was a game that only the elite were allowed to play. Government officials feared that if the peasants played the game, it would stimulate their brains and raise their intellect, thus causing them to be less happy with their meager circumstances. But the game was so popular and so interesting to play, that it soon spread throughout China among people of all classes. However, when Chairman Mao came to power in 1949, **his regime outlawed mahjong** claiming it was a capitalist game because players would sometimes gamble on the outcome. That ban didn't apply to Hong Kong, of course, because it was under British rule, so the people of Hong Kong continued to play mahjong, **making it one of their favorite pastimes.** And although some in Hong Kong gambled on mahjong, most engaged in it for the pure enjoyment of it.

Then, in 1985, China lifted its prohibition on mahjong and it has been a popular game in both Hong Kong and the mainland since then.

The 144 tiles that make up the Hong Kong version of a mahjong set are interesting. **They all have meaning and symbolism that reflect the culture, ideals, and values of China.** The three suits in the game are **bamboo, circles, and characters.** Bamboo is the most versatile plant in China, and its mahjong pieces symbolize strength, usefulness, and service. The circle pieces are associated with coins and money and they symbolize wealth, luxury, and commerce. Character tiles, each with the Chinese character for 10,000 on the lower portion of the tile, symbolize the vastness and universal nature of Chinese life. Additionally, tiles with dragons, the four winds, and flowers are part of a mahjong set (although some versions of the game don't include flowers).

The game is somewhat like gin rummy except you play it with heavy rectangular-shaped tiles instead of cards. Players noisily shuffle, draw, and discard tiles in turn until someone has assembled a mahjong – that is when all 14 tiles in your hand make up four sets plus one pair. **These tiles are then noisily slammed down on the table as the winning player loudly proclaims "mahjong."**

As depicted in Amy Tan's book *The Joy Luck Club*, a mahjong game is often an excuse for getting together with friends. In the book, three Chinese women and the daughter of a fourth woman who has passed away, gather each week as The Joy Luck Club to visit, laugh, gossip, and review their life histories – and especially to talk about their daughters. The book provides a fascinating and moving account of the intricacies of their lives – their births, marriages, marital problems, illnesses, deaths, successes, and failures – all done in the setting of a weekly gathering to play mahjong. **The book helps us see the important social and therapeutic role that mahjong can play in Chinese society.**

Sadly, mahjong played with actual tiles rather than playing it on a phone or computer, is a bit on the decline in Hong Kong. The tiles, which traditionally were made of **bamboo, bone, wood, or even ivory,** are now almost always made of hard plastic. In the past, skilled artists hand carved the symbols into each tile and then hand painted the green, blue, and red colors into the etchings. Today, nearly all mahjong sets are mass-produced by machines in factories.

Luckily, Hong Kong still has several small businesses that produce handmade sets. If you'd like to see a place where this fascinating and detailed work is done, visit the tiny shop located under a staircase at #24-A Bulkeley Street in Hung Hom on the Kowloon side. **It is called Kam Fat Mahjong and the elderly woman there, Mrs. Ho, has been carving mahjong tiles for more than 50 years.** It takes her about a week to make a full set.

If you might want to learn how to play mahjong and have some food while you are at it, go to the **Dim Sum Library Restaurant** in Pacific Place on the island. Besides offering excellent upscale dim sum, they have a mahjong parlor in the rear of the restaurant where guests can join with others to play. The restaurant also offers mahjong classes in English for those wishing to learn the game.

And did you notice that mahjong even made it into *Seinfeld*? In one episode, George Costanza's colorful mother, Estelle, is shown gossiping loudly with three of her friends as they play mahjong. The women's high-pitched chatter, incessant arguing about their husbands, and the constant slamming down of their mahjong tiles, **all help confirm that mahjong truly is the noisiest parlor game in the world.**

Written on the front of a T-shirt: I got a new mahjong set for my husband. What a trade!

Chinese Term

Thousand-Year Eggs

An age-old Chinese delicacy, thousand-year eggs were created as a way to preserve eggs for times of need rather than let them spoil. **A bit of a misnomer, they are duck eggs that have been preserved in a mixture of clay, ash, salt, and quicklime for at least 100 days, not a thousand years.** After generously coating the eggs with this mixture and rolling them in rice hulls, the eggs are buried in soil in a ceramic crock. After the proper time has elapsed, the eggs are brought out, cleaned, shelled, and eaten.

A popular street treat and restaurant side dish, many people enjoy their unusual and distinctive taste. **Eating thousand-year eggs is said to provide a number of benefits.** They:

- Improve appetite
- Have higher protein than a normal egg
- Are a good source of iron
- Act as an aphrodisiac
- Lower blood pressure
- Are low in carbohydrates

Thousand-year eggs are available in wet markets, from vendors on the street, and in many Hong Kong restaurants.

Rice

"I like rice. Rice is great if you're hungry and you want 2,000 of something." – Mich Ehrenborg (author)

My friend, Craig, asked me how my book about Hong Kong was coming along. I told him it was progressing nicely and that I presently was working on a chapter about rice. Craig responded, **"Rice? A chapter on rice? Why would anyone want to read a chapter about rice?"** Well, Craig, the Chinese people in Hong Kong are hugely interested in rice, and so am I, and so I'm going to try to write some things about rice that even you, a lifelong lover of potatoes and French fries, might find interesting.

In the earlier days of Hong Kong, rice shops offering nothing but rice were common throughout the colony. One that I was familiar with in the 1960s was near one of the apartments I lived in. **This store only sold rice – dozens of varieties of rice.** Rice was packed into containers in every corner of the shop – large barrels and bins of loose rice where the clerk would scoop up and bag the exact amount you wanted; burlap bags of rice too heavy for one person to carry; medium-sized woven baskets containing special varieties; smaller cloth or paper bags of rice you could carry under your arm or on the back of your bicycle; and small packets with only enough rice for one or two meals that could fit nicely into a shopping bag.

Simple handwritten signs in Chinese showing the type of rice and its price were mounted on sticks stuck into the piles of rice. Rice was everywhere, and when Mr. Wong, the proprietor, opened his shop in the morning, additional barrels and bags of rice from the back room would be brought out and placed on the sidewalk so that they extended clear out to the edge of the street. Passersby would have to carefully weave their way through all of these bags and containers as they made their way past his shop.

We'll get back to this rice shop later in the chapter, but first let's take a look at some things about rice, the world's most popular grain food.

- **Main Food** – Rice is the main food for over 50% of the people of the world. **Over half of the world's population eats rice three times per day,** 90% of all rice is grown and consumed in Asia, and about 94% of the world's rice is consumed in the area in which it is grown.
- **How Much per Person?** – How much rice does an average person eat? **People in China eat about 180 pounds of rice per year** compared to about 30 pounds for an average American – and that 30 pounds per year for Americans is a 25% increase compared to just two decades ago.
- **Types** – Rice is categorized into three main classifications:

- o **Long Grain** – Long grain rice is slender with a length that is four to five times its width. It is light, fluffy, and a bit drier than other varieties. **Jasmine rice is an example of a long grain rice.** It is known as an aromatic rice and has more flavor and fragrance than other types. Interestingly, most Jasmine rice eaten in Hong Kong comes from Thailand. The highest-class restaurants and the best hotels in Hong Kong serve Jasmine rice.
- o **Medium Grain** – The grains of medium grain rice are about twice as long as they are wide. Medium grain rice is tender, slightly sticky, and somewhat creamy when cooked. A rice called sweet rice is an example of a medium grain rice that is popular in Hong Kong.
- o **Short Grain** – Short grain rice is short and plump, being only slightly longer than it is wide. Short grain rice becomes soft and sticky when cooked and is often the choice when making sushi or rice pudding.
- **Wild Rice** – Contrary to what is typically believed, **wild rice is not rice at all.** It is an aquatic grass, not a grain.
- **Fried Rice** – Fried rice is a misunderstood Chinese dish. In a typical Chinese restaurant, fried rice is an entrée item that you might order for your dining group along with other entrées such as kung pao chicken, steamed fish, or beef with broccoli. **Fried rice is not ordered in place of, or as a substitute for white rice. Rather it is a main dish.** White rice is normally served as a standard part of a Chinese meal and does not have to be ordered separately.
- **Planting by Hand** – For centuries, rice has been planted by hand. Farmers perform this tedious and backbreaking chore in rice paddies – specially laid out fields that are flooded prior to the planting of the rice stalks. **Planting and harvesting rice by hand is said to be one of the most labor-intensive activities in all of agriculture.**
- **Children's Songs** – In western culture, our children's songs are about things such as the wheels on a bus (*The Wheels on the Bus Go Round and Round*), a little teapot with a spout (*I'm a Little Teapot*), or ears that hang low (*Do Your Ears Hang Low?*). In the Chinese culture, children's songs are more about practical things such as counting ducks (***Duck, Duck Count***), helping with the vegetables (***Pulling the Radish***), or toiling in the rice fields (***Planting Rice is Never Fun***). Here

is the English translation of this popular children's planting song:

Planting Rice is Never Fun
(Chinese Children's Song)

Planting rice is never fun,
Bent from morn 'til set of sun.
Cannot stand and cannot sit,
Cannot rest a little bit.

Oh, my back is like to break,
Oh, my bones with dampness ache.
And my legs are numb and set,
From the soaking in the wet.

- **Planting Rice from the Air** – The rising cost of labor has caused farmers in some parts of the world, such as in the Sacramento Valley in the U.S., to plant rice from airplanes. Low-flying single-engine crop duster planes loaded with soaked rice seeds drop the seeds onto pre-flooded fields. **The pilots are called rice jockeys.**
- **The Rice Association** – Here is a bit of a head scratcher. The headquarters of the Rice Association, the largest group of rice producers in the world, is located in England, **a country in which rice cannot be grown due to England's adverse climate.** (The rice plant requires large quantities of rainfall in its early days followed by an uninterrupted season of hot dry weather.)
- **Cooked Rice** – When cooked, most varieties of rice swell to over three times their original weight.
- **Varieties** – There are **more than 40,000 varieties** of cultivated rice. Rice can be white, yellow, golden, brown, purple, red, or black in color. Rice is commonly grown on every continent but one – Antarctica.
- **The Words for Rice** – As one might suspect, in Chinese different words in their vocabulary refer to different types and uses of rice. In Cantonese, **wòh** is rice still on the stalk growing in the field, **máih** is uncooked rice, **faahn** is cooked rice, and **jūk** is congee (a thick rice porridge).

- **Have You Eaten Yet?** – A polite way to greet someone in Hong Kong is to ask them, **"Léih sihk faahn meih a?"** which means, "Have you eaten rice yet?" Regardless of whether or not you have actually just eaten, a proper response is, **"Haih. Ngóh sihkjó faahn,"** which means, "Yes. I have already eaten rice."

- **Etiquette When Eating Rice** – What is proper etiquette concerning eating rice with chopsticks? **Woody Allen** helped us with this in the 1972 movie *Play It Again Sam*. In the film, Woody plays the role of an eccentric man whose wife has left him. Even though he resists it, Woody's friends line him up on a blind date and they go out to dinner at a Chinese restaurant called the Hong Fat Noodle Company. Woody tries to impress his date by showing her how to eat rice from a bowl with chopsticks. While lifting his bowl heaped full of rice up to the level of his mouth, he says: **"What's interesting is when Chinese eat rice with chopsticks authentically, they bring it up to their mouths in a shoveling move with their arm."** He then proceeds to push the rice towards his mouth with the chopsticks. In doing so, most of the rice misses his mouth and goes all over him, all over the table, and all over his surprised date. Even though Woody's technique was lacking, he was correct in his etiquette lesson to his blind date. **You do not need to try to pick up rice grain by grain with your chopsticks.** It is perfectly acceptable to bring your rice bowl up to your mouth and to use your chopsticks to push the rice into your mouth. And when you are done with your meal, it is good etiquette to place both chopsticks on top of your rice bowl as a sign that you are finished. But don't point the chopsticks across the table at another guest. That would be rude. And don't stick your chopsticks upright in a bowl of rice. Chopsticks stuck in a mound of rice are associated with death and funerals.

- **Rice Paper** – Rice paper is somewhat of a misnomer because most **rice paper is not made from rice.** It is made from the pith of a tree called a rice tree – which is more like a shrub than a rice plant. Rice paper is a thin edible paper used to wrap spring rolls and other Asian food. Although some rice paper is made from rice flour, the majority of rice paper is not a rice product.

- **Rice as Micro-Art Jewelry** – Artists have painted people's names and even beautiful scenes **on individual grains of rice.** The painted rice grain is then often placed in a small glass tube so it can be worn as a necklace, bracelet, or key chain.

- **Rice Bowls and Employment** – In Hong Kong, those who are jobless are often referred to as people who have **a broken rice bowl,** whereas those with secure employment are said to have **iron rice bowls.**

- **Storage Life** – The most common form of rice, white rice, can be stored up to 30 years. White rice has had the outer husk removed and the bran layers have been milled until the grain is white. Brown rice is unmilled rice. It has a shelf life of about six months.

- **Fertility Sign** – Rice is a sign of fertility and good fortune to the Chinese, a belief that has helped promote the practice in many cultures of **throwing rice above the heads of newlyweds** after the wedding ceremony to help ensure a long and happy life filled with children.

- **Pockmarks** – Hong Kong mothers sometimes warn their daughters who are finicky eaters that every grain of rice they leave in their rice bowl represents a pockmark on the face of their future husband.

- **Rice Husks** – Before rice can be eaten, the husks have to be removed from the kernel. In many countries, these rice husks are **used as fuel to help generate electricity.**

- **Rice Seed Yields** – **One little seed of rice can yield as much as 3,000 individual grains of rice,** making it the highest-yielding cereal grain. A one-pound bag of long grain rice contains more than 29,000 grains of rice.

- **A Push for Potatoes** – Concerned about land and water shortages as its 1.4 billion population continues to grow, **the Chinese government is on a campaign to convince its citizens that potatoes are an attractive alternative to eating rice.** They say that pound for pound, the potato provides more calories and vitamins per acre and uses 30% less water to grow than rice.

- **The Price of Rice in China** – And what is the answer to the commonly asked question, "And what does that have to do with the price of rice in China?" I personally have no idea, but based on World Bank figures, the price of rice in China is **US$427 per metric ton.** The all-time high price was in April

2008 (US$1,015) and the record low was in February 1983 (US$37).

Now, back to Mr. Wong's rice shop. It still is in the same place, Mr. Wong is still the proprietor, and the store still only sells rice. His loyal clientele still relies on his expertise concerning rice and they still think his rice is the best in Hong Kong. But today in Hong Kong, **the small independent stores devoted solely to selling rice have nearly disappeared,** having been replaced by larger food stores and huge supermarkets. But rice is still as important and popular as ever. Compared to just a small portion of a shelf in a U.S. supermarket being devoted to rice, entire aisles of Hong Kong's food markets and superstores offer many types of rice and a multitude of rice-based products. And the people of Hong Kong are as particular as ever about their rice, insisting on the very best varieties and the highest quality of rice for their meals.

So, Craig, I hope this chapter about rice has been of interest to you. Maybe we should do lunch. How about going out for some Chinese food? My appetite for some really good Cantonese food, including a big dish of ham fried rice, is really high at the moment.

Chinese Term

Chops

Sitting on a shelf to the left of my desk is a beautiful black and red Chinese box lined in bright red silk fabric. Nestled into a rectangular indentation in the silk sits my personal chop **(a chop is a Chinese signature seal)** and next to that in a circular recess is a blue and white porcelain container of **red cinnabar paste.** The chop itself is a piece of marble with the three characters of my Chinese name carved in mirror image into the bottom surface. Two Chinese dragons are carved on the top of the piece of marble.

If I had been a businessperson in Hong Kong in its early days, I would have used a chop, rather than a pen, to affix my name to a document in order to give it authenticity. And if I were acting in the capacity of an official of a company, I would have used a chop that bore the name and symbol of that institution, rather than my personal chop, to sign the document. **The chop on the document would have been considered more official and binding than if I had put my signature on it.**

Chops have been used in China for more than 3,000 years. Even today, chops are often used to provide an official and meaningful seal to important things – **things such as birth, marriage and death certificates, as well as wills, property deeds, important letters, and artwork.** Chops are typically carved out of stone, plastic, or wood – and even ivory was used before it was banned. Chop carvers can still be found in Hong Kong, **often conducting their small businesses in cramped booths located on side streets and in alleys.**

In addition to providing an important function in Chinese culture, **chops are beautiful pieces of artwork and many old chops are valuable collector's items.** Dozens of examples of interesting chops can be viewed on the internet by Googling **"Chinese Chops or Seals Images."**

The Golden Doll

As I got into the taxi, I asked the driver in Cantonese to take me to the Mormon Temple in Kowloon Tong. He looked a little confused, so I said it again a little more slowly. He smiled and said that he understood my Cantonese just fine, but that he was pretty sure there was no temple in Kowloon Tong. **He said that Hong Kong had lots of temples, but not one in that area.** I then told him that it was on Cornwall Street and that it had a gold Angel Moroni on top of the building. **"Oh," he said, "you want the building that has a golden doll on it. I know where that is."** About 15 minutes later we arrived at the correct destination. (Note – The church has recently begun a major renovation of the temple, which has included the removal of the Angel Moroni from the top of the building.)

From a religious beliefs standpoint, Hong Kong is a fascinating place. **There are more than 600 Buddhist and Taoist temples, many Christian churches, five mosques, three synagogues, a Hindu temple, a Sihk temple – and one Mormon temple** (see the note at end of the chapter about the correct name of the church). The people of Hong Kong are known for having **diverse religious beliefs and a high degree of religious tolerance.** The great majority of the population follows traditional Chinese religions and philosophies – **Buddhism, Taoism, Confucianism, and ancestor worship** – but many other religions including Christianity, Islam, and Hinduism are also widely practiced.

Let's take a look at some of the various religious beliefs, practices, and customs of the people of Hong Kong.

- **The Word "Religion"** – **The word "religion" did not exist in the Chinese language until relatively recently.** It wasn't until Christian missionaries brought their beliefs to China several hundred years ago, that the Chinese word for religion was created. That word in Cantonese is "jùnggaau," which combines the two characters for "to believe" and "to teach."

- **No Affiliation** – According to official statistics, **most of Hong Kong's 7.5 million people claim no affiliation with an organized religion.** Rather, they follow Chinese traditional beliefs that embrace the worship of ancestors and local gods. On surveys about religion, most Hong Kong people indicate they have no formal religion.

- **Those Who are Affiliated** – Of those who do claim an affiliation, over one million are Buddhists, another million are Taoists, 670,000 are Christians, 220,000 are Muslims, 40,000 are Hindus, and about 10,000 are Sikhs.

- **"One Country, Two Systems"** – The fact that the Chinese government allows religious freedom in Hong Kong and does not allow it in mainland China is a good example of what is meant by the **"one country, two systems"** idea of government. The People's Republic of China created the political principle of "one country, two systems" in the 1980s as part of its efforts to reunify China. **This principle says that there can only be one China, but distinct regions (such as Hong Kong) can retain their own capitalist and economic systems and ideas while the rest of China continues to use the socialist system.** As discussed in the following paragraphs, Hong Kong has religious freedom and mainland China does not.

- **Hong Kong Has Freedom of Religious Belief** – Religious freedom is one of the fundamental rights enjoyed by the people of Hong Kong. When Hong Kong was handed over to the People's Republic of China on July 1, 1997, an important law came into effect. Called the **Basic Law**, it set forth the relationship between the new Hong Kong Special Administrative Region (HKSAR) and the central government of China. The Basic Law stipulated the fundamental policies of China towards Hong Kong that were to apply after the handover. Still in effect today, the Basic Law states that the people of Hong Kong are granted **"freedom of conscience; freedom of religious belief; and freedom to preach, conduct and participate in religious activities in public."** The Basic Law also states that the government cannot interfere in the internal affairs of religious organizations or restrict religious activities which do not go against other laws. In the twenty-plus years since the handover, the Chinese government in Beijing has largely adhered to and abided by the Basic Law rules that pertain to religious beliefs in Hong Kong.

- **Mainland China Does Not Have Religious Freedom** – Mainland China, however, is a different story. The U.S. State Department's most recent International Religious Freedom Report names **sixteen nations as "Countries of Particular**

Concern" (CPCs) due to their severe violations of religious freedom. China is one of the nations on that list. According to the State Department's report, **"The Chinese government's control over religion has led to restrictions on activities and personal freedom when such activities are perceived as threatening to the Chinese Communist Party."** In mainland China, the Chinese government has actively restricted religious expression that could potentially undermine its authority.

- **Composite Religions** – Generally speaking, the majority of Hong Kong people have never established exact, formal systems of doctrines and have seldom organized their beliefs into specific churches and institutions. **So, most Hong Kong Chinese have never had to decide which church to join.** They just continue to do what their family has done for ages. Most people in Hong Kong have adopted a composite religious viewpoint – **usually a blending of Buddhism, Taoism, Confucianism, and ancestor worship.**

- **Practical Beliefs** – Most Hong Kong Chinese are a practical people when it comes to their beliefs. They tend to follow the god or gods that will do them the most personal good. They have gods that specialize in all sorts of things – cooking, fishing, farming, longevity, prosperity, etc. **If worshiping a particular god seems to help, then they keep worshiping it. If not, they change gods.** They have little time for gods that are powerless or ones that cannot aid them. Chinese people are mainly concerned with the help that gods can give them in everyday situations, not with theology and doctrine.

- **Buddhism** – Although Buddhism is often associated with China, it actually originated in southern Nepal and northern India about 500 B.C. It is now widely practiced in mainland China and Hong Kong. As taught by Buddha, the essence of Buddhism is contained in the Four Noble Truths and the Noble Eightfold Path.

The Four Noble Truths are:
1. Life is suffering
2. The origin of suffering is desire
3. Suffering ends when we eliminate desire
4. The Eightfold Path casts out desire

The Noble Eightfold Path is:
1. Right belief
2. Right purpose
3. Right speech
4. Right conduct
5. Right means of livelihood
6. Right effort
7. Right mindfulness
8. Right meditation

- **Taoism** – Founded by Chinese philosopher Lao Tzu during the 4th century B.C., Taoism teaches about harmony and perfection in life. When things are allowed to take their natural course and when **the tao (the way or path)** is followed, things develop and progress properly and harmony is achieved. The concept of **yin and yang** is of Taoist origin. Many people in mainland China, and around one million residents of Hong Kong, subscribe to this philosophy.

- **Confucianism** – The teachings of Confucius have had a major impact for several thousand years on the thinking and culture of Chinese people, both in mainland China and in Hong Kong. **Confucianism is largely a system of ethics rather than a religion.** Confucius taught that all should strive to be superior human beings and his mission was to help his followers understand the principles involved in becoming so. **His students spent most of the latter part of his life writing and compiling his thoughts and wise sayings** into books that have played an influential role in the history of China and in the thinking of many of the people of Hong Kong.

- **Ancestor Worship** – The Chinese have a deep appreciation for their roots and **believe it is essential to pay proper homage and devotion to their ancestors, whose spirits they believe remain alive after death.** They do this by keeping extensive genealogical records and by performing sacrifices to their ancestors. They believe that if deceased family members are honored and treated properly, they will use their spiritual powers to guide and bless their living descendants in their earthly pursuits. It is not unusual to see altars, ancestral shrines, or god shelves containing various pictures, candles, and religious objects in many homes and businesses. Here, incense is burned and fruit, food, and other items are offered to the deceased. When asked why they do this, many just say this is the way their family has worshiped for as long as they can remember and that it is how they pay honor and respect. Through offering up their sacrifices, they hope to win the approval of their ancestors so that their life will be happy and prosperous.

- **Christianity** – Christianity is common among both the ethnic Chinese as well as the foreigners who live in Hong Kong. **Christian churches have been in Hong Kong since the early days of British rule (since 1841),** and have played a major role in helping feed, clothe, house, educate, and provide medical services for the thousands upon thousands of Chinese who have sought asylum and have come across the border from China to Hong Kong over the years.

- **Many Religious Events and Festivals are Public Holidays** – A number of public holidays are tied to traditional Chinese festivals and the various religious beliefs of the people of Hong Kong. Official days off for Hong Kong workers include the Chinese New Year Festival (three days), the Ching Ming Festival, Buddha's birthday, the Tuen Ng Festival, the Mid-Autumn Festival, and the Chung Yeung Festival. Additionally, the Christian events of Good Friday, Easter Monday, and Christmas are also public holidays.

Religious freedom and the right of religious belief help make Hong Kong a culturally rich and highly interesting place. Under the terms of the 1997 handover agreement, these basic rights are guaranteed to be protected until at least 2047.

(Note – The correct name of the Mormon Church is **The Church of Jesus Christ of Latter-day Saints.** The word **"Mormon"** and the letters **"LDS"** are often used by non-members of the church in place of the full name. Both are nicknames for the church, which has over 22,000 members and approximately 150 full-time missionaries in Hong Kong. My two times living in Hong Kong were as a representative for the church – first as a 19-year-old missionary for two-and-a half years and then with my wife for three years as we supervised the missionary work of the church's China Hong Kong Mission.)

Chinese Term

Dim Sum

The lights were too bright at the Chinese restaurant, so the manager decided to dim sum. (That's the only joke I know about Chinese food.) Meaning touching the heart (or small heart), **dim sum refers to food delicacies that are brought to your table in small portions in bamboo steamer baskets or on small plates.** Although dim sum is served throughout China and is available in many Chinese restaurants outside of China (especially in Chinatowns), **the Cantonese people in Hong Kong are acknowledged as the true masters of this food form.** Going out for dim sum (or going to yum cha as it is also known) is part of a daily ritual for many in Hong Kong and **is a must for any tourist visiting there.** Available in the late morning and early afternoon at many restaurants, eating dim sum with friends is a popular pastime after completing exercises or visiting the morning market. Some favorite dim sum foods are:

- **Har Gow** – Steamed dumplings in a light translucent wrap that conceals shrimp and bamboo shoots.
- **Pai Gwat** – Bite-size pieces of succulent spare ribs in a black bean and chili pepper sauce.
- **Siu Mai** – Steamed pork dumplings.
- **Gai Jaht** – Chicken and ham wrapped in soya been sheets served in a rich sauce.
- **Cheong Fan** – Rolls of rice pastry filled with shrimp, pork, or beef smothered in a sweet soy sauce.
- **Gai Geuk** – Chicken feet.
- **Daan Taat** – Egg tarts with a custard filling.

- **Char Siu Bao** – Steamed pork buns.

Each dim sum is normally small in size, with three or four pieces on each dish. It is customary to share the dishes with the others at your table.

An excellent place in Hong Kong for dim sum is Maxim's Palace located in City Hall on the island. Here, servers wheel the selections past your table on trolleys. As the trolley arrives, ask the server to lift the lid of the bamboo basket so you can take a peek at what dim sum item is being offered. If you want some, just give a nod and it will be placed on your table. Each size of plate costs a certain price, and when you are finished, they will count up the plates on your table and tally your bill.

Psst...Wanna Buy Some Golf Clubs?

Shopping in Hong Kong is a lot of fun. When we lived there, we often went to Mong Kok (located on the Kowloon Peninsula) to check out the amazing bargains found there. **Mong Kok is a jam-packed place where you can shop for nearly everything you can think of.** In fact, entire streets in the Mong Kok area are devoted to a single type of product, such as:

- **Ladies Street (Tung Choi Street)** – an amazing number of shops and booths specializing in women's clothing, jewelry, purses, shoes, cosmetics, and a variety of other items
- **Sneakers Street (Fa Yuen Street)** – a host of small retail shops selling running shoes, sports equipment, and sports clothing
- **Bird Street (Yuen Po Street)** – a long line of shops with birds, bird cages, and pet supplies
- **Flower Market Road (Prince Edward Road)** – this street, and the nearby side streets, are packed with vendors and florist shops selling flowers and plants of all varieties
- **Electronics Street (Sai Yeung Choi Street)** – dozens of shops selling consumer electronic products, computers, phones, games, watches, and cameras

- **Goldfish Street (Tung Choi Street)** – an entire street of hawkers and shops selling tropical freshwater fish, marine fish, and aquarium accessories
- **Kitchenware Street (Shanghai Street)** – a slew of stores selling products for home and commercial kitchens
- **Tile Street (Portland Street)** – more than 50 stores selling tile, countertops, wall paper, bath tubs, toilets, and sinks

Even though much of the merchandise in Mong Kok is legitimate, **it is also a haven for knock-offs and fake brand-name products.** So, when I decided to buy a new set of golf clubs, I avoided Mong Kok and its bargains and instead went to the Star Ferry area of Kowloon where a number of golf shops are located. I wanted to make sure my clubs were not knock-offs, so I only went to shops displaying signs indicating that they were authorized dealers for the top brands of golf equipment such as Titleist, Callaway, Mizuno, and TaylorMade. Then I began the enjoyable process of looking at golf equipment and seeing what kind of a deal I could come up with – because I love bargaining in Hong Kong.

I took extra precautions when buying the clubs because of the horror stories I had heard about fake golf equipment. One such story involved a friend of mine who purchased a brand-name set of clubs in a foreign country he was visiting. The first time he used them, he noticed that the sound that the driver made when it hit the ball was kind of different. Before the end of his first round, the head of the club had worked its way loose and had fallen off. Although he had saved several hundred dollars, **the clubs were knock-offs and his purchase was a waste of good money.**

Some of the problems commonly associated with knock-off golf equipment and what might happen when you play with them are:

- **Problem** – Cheap and inferior adhesives are used to connect the various parts
  - o **Result** – Heads fall off, heads twist on the shafts, grips come loose
- **Problem** – Heads are not manufactured properly, causing the sizes and lofts of the heads to be off

- o **Result** – Clubs are inconsistent, balls come off the club head at wrong angles, accuracy is decreased, shots are erratic, the clubs in a set of irons are improperly matched with each other

- • **Problem** – Use of inferior or substitute materials
  - o **Result** – Distance is compromised, driver heads don't perform as designed, sweet spots are not per spec, solid hits are less frequent, grips don't feel right and deteriorate rapidly, shafts bend, warp, or shatter
- • **Problem** – Graphics are cheap and incomplete
  - o **Result** – Colors are bland and not per spec, labels are not attached properly, graphics fade and are hard to read, words are spelled incorrectly

The U.S. Golf Manufacturers Anti-Counterfeiting Working Group says:

> **"It is estimated that as many as 2 million counterfeit golf clubs are produced each year.** To put that number in perspective, if you laid every fake club end-to-end they would stretch from Bethpage Black (in New York) to Pebble Beach (in California) and back again. And that doesn't even take into account the millions of fake balls, bags, gloves, and apparel produced."

The organization then goes on to say that **up to 95% of fake golf clubs are sold through internet sites** or by small shops in foreign countries that are not approved golf dealers. Several of the major golf manufacturers have warnings on their web sites about fake golf products. For example, here is the warning from Callaway Golf:

> **"Counterfeit Club Warning.** To protect our valued customers from fraud, Callaway Golf shares the following warning: Consumers all around the world have been duped into purchasing so-called 'brand new, authentic Callaway Golf products' at very low prices on eBay.com and other internet auction and online retail sites that have turned out to actually be low-quality fakes. Sales of counterfeit Callaway Golf products on such sites have dramatically increased over the last few years."

So, here are a few thoughts to consider when purchasing golf equipment **in order to help steer clear of knock-offs:**

- Only buy golf equipment from authorized dealers.
- If the price seems too good to be true, it probably is too good to be true. Don't make the purchase.
- Does the seller say the price for the brand-new equipment is at a low bargain-basement level because "the clubs were a gift I didn't need" or "I won the clubs in a tournament or raffle?" If so, be extremely cautious. Sellers often use these types of stories to con their victims.
- If you are in doubt about a potential purchase, call or email the purported manufacturer of the golf equipment before

committing to the transaction. They will be glad to help you know if the clubs are theirs and if they are authentic.

- Be extra cautious when purchasing golf equipment on the internet. Even reputable sites may unknowingly be selling counterfeit items.
- Be careful about sending money to people you don't know. This is especially true when buying golf equipment from an overseas source. If the equipment you have purchased is counterfeit, it may be confiscated by U.S. Customs as it arrives in our country, and if so, you'll never even see the equipment – and good luck with trying to get your money back.
- Take the time to carefully study the equipment you are planning to purchase. Look at the smallest details. Then compare the club with the identical piece of equipment available at an authorized dealer. Most brand-name golf manufacturers do not sell clubs that are seconds or have blemishes, so if you see any discrepancies, even small ones, the equipment you are planning to purchase may be counterfeit.
- If you do end up with counterfeit equipment, report what happened to the internet site, if it was purchased online, as well as to the manufacturer whose name appears on the clubs.

It has now been several years and I am still enjoying the set of clubs I purchased in Hong Kong. **They are excellent and have really helped my golf game.** I am happy that I was able to bargain a bit and save a little money on them when I made the purchase.

(Note – This chapter was first published in the author's book *Golfing – A View Through the Golf Hole.*)

148

Chinese Term

Skyscraper

Although the Chinese didn't invent the word skyscraper (originally the word skyscraper was an English nautical term), the Chinese certainly have become experts at building them. **The word skyscraper derives from a special sail on old-time sailing ships.** During times when the wind was unusually light, a sailing vessel would often raise **a lightweight triangular-shaped sail called a skyscraper** high above the other sails in order to catch every breath of wind available.

In Cantonese, a skyscraper is a mōtìn daaihhah, **a touch-the-sky building.** And do you know which city in the world has the most skyscrapers? Dubai, New York City, Hong Kong, Rio, London? Because this is a book about Hong Kong, **you probably should have picked Hong Kong as the answer,** especially if you've already read Chapter 3. And if you chose Hong Kong, you would have been correct. Hong Kong has 26% more skyscrapers than New York City, the city that comes in second.

The Council on Tall Buildings and Urban Habitat (CTBUH) is the international body that certifies the height of the world's buildings and issues various lists related to the world's tallest buildings. According to the CTBUH, a building is categorized as a skyscraper if its height is **150 meters and above** (150 meters equates to about 492 feet). From their most recent list, here are the cities with the most skyscrapers, with three of the top five and six of the top 10 being in China:

1. **Hong Kong, China – 355 skyscrapers**
2. New York City, USA – 282
3. Shenzhen, China – 270
4. Dubai, UAE – 199
5. Shanghai, China – 163
6. Tokyo, Japan – 155
7. Chongqing, China – 127
8. Chicago, USA – 126
9. Guangzhou, China – 115
10. Wuhan, China – 96

Because they are packed into such a small and compact area, Hong Kong's 355 skyscrapers are an especially interesting sight, particularly when viewed from Victoria Peak or from the Kowloon side of the harbor.

I love going to tall buildings. Holly and I have had the opportunity of visiting a number of the tallest buildings in the world, even receiving a special personal tour of the tallest one, the Burj Khalifa at 2,717 feet, when we were traveling in Dubai. **Wow, what a building that is!** It is the tallest one in the world by a huge margin, **reaching 644 feet higher** than the one in second place, the Shanghai Tower in Shanghai, China. And how does the Burj Khalifa compare to the Empire State Building in New York City, which once was the tallest building in the world? The Burj Khalifa is more than twice as tall as the Empire State Building.

All skyscrapers are magnificent, but of the ones I've seen, **my favorite skyscrapers by far are the ones located in Hong Kong – all 355 of them.**

Amazing Bamboo

A story about bamboo that I heard many years ago from some Chinese friends **gives us insight into how Chinese and westerners differ** in their approach to understanding the things around them and in how they view life in general.

Understanding Bamboo

A Chinese scholar was seeking enlightenment about the essence of bamboo. There were many bamboo plants growing near his small village and he desired to better understand this interesting plant and its essential characteristics so he could appreciate it more. In order to acquire this knowledge, the scholar decided to sit in a bamboo grove and carefully observe bamboo until he understood it. Day after day, he sat in the grove and focused himself on the bamboo surrounding him as it rustled in the wind and grew taller. **After a week of careful observation, he left the grove, having gained an understanding of the plant.**

In another part of the world, a western scientist was also studying bamboo. He wanted to come to an understanding of this unusual plant so that he could put it to its best use. He cut off a bamboo plant and took it into his lab. There, under bright lights, he sawed the stalk in two, separated the leaves from the stem, and began studying the plant. **After a week of cutting, dissecting, and looking at it under a microscope, he left his lab, having gained an understanding of the plant.**

The Chinese scholar reached the conclusion that the essence of bamboo is that it has hollow segments, just as a man should have an open mind and an open heart; that it is upright and rigid against the outside pressures of the world, as a proper man should be; and that it grows green and fresh despite the environment, just as an enlightened person should do.

The western scientist reached the conclusion that bamboo is one of twelve subfamilies in the grass family Poaceae; that its main components are rhizomes, roots, culms, branches, leaves, and flowers; that its culm, or stem, is hollow and that the vascular bundles in the cross-section are scattered throughout the stem instead of in a cylindrical fashion; and that its leaves are distinguished by the presence of well-developed asymmetrically strong invaginated arm cells.

As this story about bamboo illustrates, **the Chinese tend to look more at the whole picture and to focus on the meaning of things while westerners move more quickly, placing a strong emphasis on efficiency and details.** The Chinese seek to establish a harmonious relationship with their environment whereas westerners seek to change and improve things. (In this regard, however, it should be noted that the people of Hong Kong are an interesting blend of the two cultures. Having been influenced by the British for over 150 years, they are both Chinese and western in the way they look at things and in how they act.)

Now let's take a closer look at this interesting plant called bamboo and the various roles it plays in Hong Kong.

The Plant and Its Uses

Bamboo is an amazing plant. It is a grass that grows from seed, but interestingly, for the first several years of the plant's growth, it forms a large system of underground roots rather than grow up out of the ground. **Then, three to five years after it is planted, it begins to put forth vertical shoots and becomes one of the fastest-growing woody plants in the world.** In the right soil and with the right growing conditions, it can grow at a rate of up to 36 inches in 24 hours. **It is one of the few plants where you can actually watch the growth take place.** At maturity, the plant can easily reach 40 or 50 feet in height. Unlike trees, individual bamboo shoots emerge from the ground at their full diameter and grow to their full height in a single growing season.

All parts of the bamboo plant – the roots, culms, branches, and leaves – are used by the people of Hong Kong in a variety of ways. They eat it (bamboo shoots in stir fry dishes and spring rolls); eat with it (bamboo chopsticks); sit on it (bamboo stools and chairs); make music with it (bamboo flutes and drums); drink it (bamboo beverages); wear it (bamboo cloth, hats, and jewelry); play with it (mahjong tiles); fish with it (bamboo fishing rods); cook in it (bamboo steamers for dim sum); cook with it (bamboo kitchen utensils); put flowers in it (bamboo vases); clean with it (bamboo brooms); live in it (houses with bamboo walls, floors, and roofs); write with it (bamboo calligraphy pens and brushes); cure diseases with it (bamboo extract used in potions); fight with it (bamboo bows, arrows, and spears); heat with it (bamboo fuel and briquets); do math with it (bamboo abacuses); ride on it (bamboo bicycle frames); and wrap food in its leaves (steamed glutinous rice dumplings). **And the pandas in Hong Kong love it!** Bamboo is the main food for the giant pandas in Hong Kong's Ocean Park located on the back side of the island.

All these uses for bamboo, and literally hundreds of others, are common in Hong Kong.

Bamboo Scaffolding

Then there is Hong Kong's world-famous bamboo scaffolding. Known as the last frontier of bamboo scaffolding, Hong Kong uses it not only as new buildings are being built **(the record highest use is on an 80-story one)**, but on old structures that are being repaired. **Hong Kong is the recognized expert in this area, having turned the erecting of bamboo scaffolding into not only an important construction craft, but also into an art form.**

Hong Kong even has a prestigious title for bamboo scaffolding experts. These craftsmen hold the prized designation of **Bamboo Scaffolding Masters.** (In Chinese culture, a master is a highly respected person who holds an important teacher-student relationship with those in their craft – **think of Master Shifu in the *Kung Fu Panda* films.**) These highly talented and valued bamboo scaffolding masters are the ones who teach the workers the details of the art and supervise the work as the scaffolding is being erected and dismantled.

No matter where you are in Hong Kong, you will probably see bamboo scaffolding in use. **Compared to metal scaffolding:**

- It is more flexible and adaptable
- It is easier to erect
- It is lighter to transport
- It is less expensive
- It is as strong
- It can be erected many times faster using the same number of workers
- It can better withstand heavy storms and typhoons
- It is readily available

And it looks really cool. If you have a spare hour, pick a comfortable place to sit across from a building where a bamboo scaffolding erection project is underway and watch what goes on. It is fascinating to see the busy workers climbing up, scampering around, and hanging off the intricate bamboo web as the scaffolding rises. After the scaffolding is in place, a green mesh material is wrapped around the entire structure, forming a type of cocoon to keep construction debris and dirt in – and to keep weather out. **(If you want to see a really interesting video about this, go to YouTube and watch the 3-minute and 51-second clip called *How it Works – Bamboo Scaffolding*.)**

Whether viewed in the Chinese way or the western way, or both, bamboo is an interesting and essential part of Hong Kong. **Bamboo truly is an amazing plant!**

Chinese Term

Ketchup – The All-American Condiment that Comes from China

Ketchup, the all-American condiment found in 97% of all U.S. kitchens, comes from China. **The word kéjāp, meaning tomato sauce or tomato paste, comes from Cantonese.** It has been a popular sauce in China and other Asian countries for many hundreds of years. The story goes that English sea traders doing business in China fell in love with the taste of the sauce and brought it back to their home country in the early 1800s. And as Englishmen immigrated to America, ketchup came with them.

Heinz, which sells over 650 million bottles of ketchup a year, is the world-wide leader in tomato ketchup with a 60% market share in the U.S. and over an 80% share in the United Kingdom. **Heinz purposely spells its product "ketchup" so as to differentiate it from others who spell it "catsup."**

Heinz suggests that the best way to get the ketchup to run out of their narrow-neck bottles is to **tap the neck** rather than thump the bottom. Smacking the bottom of the bottle will loosen up the ketchup in the bottom area, but it has little effect on the sauce in the neck of the bottle – and it is the ketchup in the neck of the bottle that needs to get loosened up. **They say that when the neck is properly tapped, the ketchup in the bottle will begin to flow naturally – at a maximum speed of 147 feet per hour.**

Oh, and do you recall what President Richard Nixon's favorite breakfast was? **It was cottage cheese with ketchup on it.** Personally, I like grilled cheese sandwiches with ketchup on them. And I once saw a Chinese person putting ketchup on rice. **To each his own.**

The Living Tractor of China

Pearl Buck's outstanding book *The Good Earth* contains a moving account on pages 50 and 51 about the water buffalo (referred to as an ox in the book) owned by Wang Lung and his wife O-lan. A severe drought has hit China and Wang Lung, a simple farmer, has run out of food for his family as well as for the beloved water buffalo that has been with him in his fields even before he married O-lan.

"Month passed into month and still no rain fell. **There came a day when there was no rice left and no wheat left and there were only a few beans and a meager store of corn, and the ox lowed with its hunger.**"

"Wang Lung's aged father then said, **'We will eat the ox, next.'** Then Wang Lung cried out, for it was to him as though one said, 'We will eat a man.' The ox was his companion in the fields and he had walked behind and praised it and cursed it as his mood was, and from his youth he had known the beast, when they had bought it as a small calf."

"The old man then said, **'Well, and it is your life or the beast's, and your son's life or the beast's.'** But Wang Lung would not that day kill it. And the next day passed and the next and the children cried out for food and they would not be comforted and O-lan looked at Wang Lung, beseeching him for the children, **and he saw at last that the thing was to be done.** So he said roughly, **'Let it be killed then, but I cannot**

do it.' He went into the room where he slept and he laid himself upon the bed and he wrapped the quilt about his head that he might not hear the beast's bellowing when it died. Then O-lan crept out and she took a great iron knife she had in the kitchen and she cut a great gash in the beast's neck, and thus she severed its life."

Water buffaloes have played an important role in mainland China for thousands of years – and in Hong Kong's New Territories and other rural areas of Hong Kong for hundreds of years. They are a wonderful animal. Water buffaloes are slow, headstrong, and stubborn as they plough the fields and carry burdens, yet they are hardworking and faithful, ideally suited for working in rice paddies. **Some have referred to the water buffalo as the living tractor of China.**

As I have observed water buffaloes over the years, I've found them to be fascinating animals, with there being more to them than one might suspect. Here are a few random items of information about them:

- There are more than **23 million** water buffaloes in China. That's equal to the human population of Australia – and a little less than the human population of Texas. Hong Kong used to have several thousand water buffaloes, but today there are only about 120 left. As housing and industrial developments have mushroomed in Hong Kong's New Territories, farms and water buffaloes have been pushed aside to the point where the farms and the water buffaloes have nearly disappeared. Most of the remaining water buffaloes are now located on Lantau Island where a group of citizens have formed the **Lantau Buffalo Association** to help protect and care for them.

- **Water buffaloes do not have any upper teeth.** They have a full row of bottom teeth, but they lack a matching set on top. They are vegetarians and chew their cud.
- The water buffalo is perfectly adapted for working in the deep mud of rice paddies **because of their wide, split hooves and flexible foot joints.** Their splayed hoof helps keep them from sinking too deeply in the mud.
- They are massive animals with barrel chests, short legs, and crescent-shaped, backward-curving horns that can stretch to as much as five feet in length.
- A water buffalo is often **a Chinese farmer's greatest capital asset.**
- China and Southeast Asia are not the only parts of the world that have water buffaloes. They also can be found in North America, Australia, and Europe.
- In Italy, water buffalo milk is used in the making of authentic mozzarella cheese. Italians call this cheese **mozzarella di bufala (buffalo mozzarella).** The U.S. imports more than 90,000 pounds of mozzarella di bufala each year.
- Worldwide, more human beings depend on the water buffalo than on any other domestic animal.
- In China, **a water buffalo is treated as a member of the family** and tending the family's water buffalo is commonly the responsibility of the children. They are the ones who often lead (or ride) the animal to the field and it is the children's job to clean any accumulated mud out of the ears and nose of the ox after it has toiled in the rice paddy.
- **Water buffaloes normally move very slowly,** with an average walking speed of only a few miles per hour – but they make up for that by being steady. In spite of their usual slowness, they have the ability to run quite fast over short distances. In some Asian countries, such as Thailand and

Indonesia (not in China), racing water buffaloes is a favorite sport.

- **Over 10% of the world's milk supply is water buffalo milk.** Water buffalo milk has 16% higher protein than cow's milk, 9% more calcium, and 37% more iron. Water buffalo milk is also lower in cholesterol than cow's milk.

- **The Double 8 Dairy in West Petaluma, California** (north of San Francisco in Sonoma County) has a herd of water buffaloes. This dairy is known for its buffalo milk as well as for **buffalo milk gelato.** The gelato is said to be extra-delicious and is especially creamy and smooth.

- Yaks and water buffaloes are distant cousins. **Both are large bovids,** which is the biological family that includes cattle, sheep, goats, and antelopes. All male bovids have horns and in some bovid species the female also has them. Yaks have long hair and typically live in cold conditions while water buffaloes have short hair and live in hot and humid locations.

- **Water buffaloes have even played a role in the TV series** *M*A*S*H.* In one episode, Hawkeye is placed under house arrest for punching Frank, the inept and disliked acting camp commander of the M*A*S*H unit. Without Frank's knowledge, **the cook slips Hawkeye a water buffalo steak as a special reward for what he did,** much to the delight of the others in the camp.

- **And do you remember the Loyal Order of Water Buffalo Lodge No. 26?** That's the one that Fred Flintstone and Barney Rubble belonged to during the six years that the *Flintstones* ran on TV.

- **As I was writing this chapter, I wondered about the correct pluralization of water buffalo.** I found that the plural can be written any of three ways – water buffaloes, water buffalos, or water buffalo. The spelling guide I use gives preference to **water buffaloes,** so that is what I have gone with in this book. And what is the plural of water buffalo in Chinese? The singular and plural of water buffalo are the same since Chinese nouns are not singular or plural. Chinese relies on context to note whether one or more than one is intended. It is not the noun itself that is singular or plural but rather the words before it that determine how many are meant.

As *The Good Earth* story continues, the rains eventually return and Wang Lung, O-lan, their children, and the old man barely survive the famine. **And as their life begins to return to normal, one of the first things Wang Lung desires is a new water buffalo.** He sees one in another farmer's field, and on page 100 of the book we read:

> "Wang Lung had been struck with its strong neck, and noticed at once the sturdy pulling of its shoulder against the wooden yoke. **Upon this ox he had set his heart because of its sturdy pulling of the soil and because of its smooth coat and its full dark eye.** With this ox he could plough his fields and cultivate them and with this ox tied to his mill he could grind the grain."

Wang Lung wants to own this fine water buffalo and enters into negotiations with the farmer for the animal:

> **"It seemed to Wang Lung as if out of all the oxen the world held he must have this one.** At last after bickering and quarreling and false starts away, the farmer yielded for half again the worth of an ox in those parts. **But gold was suddenly nothing to Wang Lung when he looked at this ox,** and he passed the money over to the farmer's hand and he watched while the farmer unyoked the beast, and Wang Lung led it away with a rope through its nostrils, **his heart burning with his possession."**

Such is the importance and meaning to a Chinese farmer of a water buffalo – **the living tractor of China.**

Chinese Term

Typhoon

Located on the edge of the South China Sea in a humid subtropical climate, Hong Kong is a prime target for typhoons. **A typhoon is the name used in the Asia region of the globe for an intense tropical storm with powerful winds and heavy rain.** If the same storm were to take place in the Atlantic Ocean area it would be called a hurricane and if it had originated in the South Pacific or Indian Ocean, it would be called a cyclone. The only difference between a typhoon, hurricane, and cyclone is the location of the world where the storm occurs. All of them are huge rotating tropical storm systems that start at sea. **Typhoon is a Cantonese word that means big wind.**

Tropical storms and typhoons are significant events in Hong Kong. Because they happen rather frequently and can cause major damage and even death, when the government's weather agency, **the Hong Kong Observatory,** issues a typhoon warning, everyone pays attention.

Some historians say that Hong Kong's most severe **actual** typhoon took place in the summer of 1937. Called the Great Typhoon, it was so strong that meteorological instruments couldn't measure it accurately, thus the technical severity of it compared to modern storms is unknown. **Accounts of the storm say that small fish were lifted out of the harbor and deposited on the roofs of a number of Hong Kong's buildings.**

Perhaps the largest and most destructive typhoon in Hong Kong's history, however, was a **fictional** one. **It took place in the James Clavell novel *Tai-Pan*.** Set in Hong Kong in the 1840s, it tells the story of Dirk Struan, the colony's most powerful businessman (known as the Tai-Pan), whose empire was dealt a major blow when he was killed as the city took a direct hit from a typhoon. A 1986 movie based on the book starred Bryan Brown as the Tai-Pan. **(Interestingly, Sean Connery turned down the role.)** *Tai-Pan* was the first English language movie shot in China.

The Name Stuck

Twinkie, Apple, Milk, Onion, and Salad. All foods we eat. Right? Not quite. **Rambo, Hiawatha, Nike, Adolf, and Caesar.** All famous historical figures. Right? Not quite. **Caramel, Cowboy, Coupon, Chocolate, and Cello.** All things in our lives starting with the letter "C." Right? Not quite. All of these are examples of **interesting first names** used by various Hong Kong people we have

met or heard about over the years. (When we lived there, my wife started keeping a list.) With China becoming more global and with western culture playing a bigger part in the lives of Chinese people, **many Chinese who were born with traditional Chinese names are picking up western first names as well.** This is especially the case in Hong Kong where both Chinese and English are the official languages and where the British influence played such a large role for more than 150 years until the 1997 handover. To help explain and better understand the when, why, and where of these western names, let's look at some specific examples:

- **Chan Kong Sang** – This particular Mr. Chan (note that in traditional Chinese names, the first word is the surname), is better known as **Jackie Chan.** With a star on the Hollywood Walk of Fame as well as on Hong Kong's Avenue of the Stars, Jackie Chan is a world-famous martial artist and movie star. Born in Hong Kong, Chan went to Australia in 1976 at the age of 22. While attending college and working construction there, he had a coworker named Jack who befriended him and took him under his wing. **Chan Kong Sang soon became known as Little Jack, which was later shortened to Jackie. The name stuck.**

- **Lee Jun Fan** – Known professionally as **Bruce Lee,** Lee Jun Fan was considered to be one of the most influential martial arts fighters of all time. Although people think of Bruce Lee as a Hong Kong person because he grew up there, he was born at the Chinese Hospital in San Francisco's Chinatown in 1940. His parents gave him the official Chinese name of Lee Jun Fan at that time – and then the attending physician at the hospital, Dr. Mary Glover, told the parents **that it would be best if their new baby boy also had an English name.** The parents agreed, so Dr. Glover added the name **Bruce** to the birth certificate. **The name stuck.**

- **Ma Yun** – Ma Yun (**Jack Ma**) is the 20th richest person in the world. He is the co-founder of the Alibaba Group, a world-wide internet-based conglomerate. Born in Hangzhou, China, Ma Yun as a boy hung around a hotel in his city that catered to foreign tourists. Wanting to learn English, Ma Yun gave free city tours to hotel guests. One of the guests really liked the young boy and became a pen pal with him, but he told Ma Yun that his Chinese name was too hard to pronounce correctly – **and that he was going to call him Jack from then on.** Jack liked the name, and **the name stuck.**

- **Yip Chi Ying** – I once heard of a young Hong Kong woman, Miss Yip, who had quite an unusual first name. Her formal name was Yip Chi Ying, but she also had a western name that was chosen by her mother. Feeling that her daughter would benefit from a western name as she started school, **the mother opened up an English dictionary and picked the first word she saw. The word was doodle.** So today, Yip Chi Ying is known among her friends as **Doodle Yip.** And Doodle loves her name, **so the name stuck.**

Sometimes a western name is chosen at or near the time of birth and sometimes not until later on. **And, of course, not all Chinese people, select a western first name.** Chairman Mao is **Mao Ze Dong,** the 7'6" former Houston Rockets pro basketball player Yao Ming is simply **Yao Ming,** the musician whose Chinese name is Ma Yo Yo is known worldwide as **Yo Yo Ma,** and Confucius is just **Confucius.** None of them has a western first name. Some Chinese people value tradition and don't approve of picking up an additional name while others think it is perfectly okay to do so. And, it should be noted so I don't paint a skewed picture, **most western first names among the Hong Kong Chinese are just regular, normal names, not unusual ones like the ones we mentioned at the start of the chapter.** As I write this comment, I am thinking of some of our good Hong Kong friends and their first names – friends like Eric Lam (Lam Ho Ming), Rita Chan (Chan Lai Yin), Stephanie Kwok (Kwok Sin Ting), Wesley Wong (Wong Hil Chun), and Joseph Lee (Lee Tin Wai). They all have added what I would call normal western first names to their regular Chinese names.

Surnames

And just a few thoughts about Chinese surnames. When it comes to surnames, the Chinese keep it a lot simpler than we do in the west. According to figures from the Chinese Academy of Sciences and the U.S. Census Bureau, **just 100 surnames cover 90% of the people in China whereas in the U.S. it takes 150,000 surnames to cover 90% of the population.** The surnames Wong, Lee, and Chan are among the most common ones of China's 1.4 billion people, with more than 93 million people being named Wong, 92 million named Lee, and 88 million named Chan. In comparison, the most common U.S. surname, Smith, covers only 2.5 million people in our country. Over 50% of all Chinese people have one of only nine Chinese family names.

And when a Chinese surname is written in English, keep in mind that it might be spelled in several different ways. For example, the surname Wong might be spelled Wong, Wang, or Wing; Lee might be Lee, Li, or Lei; and Chan might be Chan, Chen, Chin, or Chun.

Chinese Term

Wok

A wok is a critical piece of cooking equipment found in virtually every kitchen in Hong Kong. In fact, a Hong Kong kitchen typically would have several woks among their array of pots and pans. With a rounded bottom as its most distinguishing feature, woks are usually made of carbon steel or cast iron, although aluminum ones are also popular.

The most common use of a wok in Hong Kong is to stir fry Cantonese dishes quickly over high heat. Woks are also used for steaming, stewing, braising, roasting, and boiling.

Although woks are available for purchase all over Hong Kong, if you're up for an interesting and adventurous buying experience, **head to Shanghai Street in the Yau Ma Tei section of Kowloon.** Also known as Kitchenware Street, Shanghai Street has rows of shops selling culinary equipment. The shops are amazing, exhibiting shelf after shelf and pile upon pile of everything needed for a well-equipped kitchen. **Besides woks of every size and shape, you'll find such traditional Chinese cooking items as bamboo steaming baskets, heavy wooden chopping blocks, meat cleavers, and extra-long bamboo chopsticks (for stirring food in large woks and pots).**

As you stroll past the many old shops along this street, be aware that the land you are walking on used to be sea. In 1874, the area now including Shanghai Street was one of the first land reclamation projects in the old British Colony of Hong Kong.

Grandma's Gift of Jade

"Gold has value. Jade is invaluable."
– An old Chinese saying

A Chinese grandmother's special gift to her newborn grandchild is often a jade bracelet. Rich in symbolism, jade is associated with good health, long life, and protection from evil spirits. Valued even more than gold, silver, and diamonds, jade is a Hong Kong person's favorite gemstone. It can be found everywhere in Hong Kong – in jewelry stores, markets, antique shops, and department stores. Because it is such an important part of Chinese culture, it would be unusual for a Chinese person not to own at least one piece of jade.

That has not always been the case. The Chinese love of jade is as old as Chinese civilization, **but originally only the powerful rulers and elite were able to own it.** As the years went by, jade objects became more and more available to the general populace, who, like the rich, prized jade for the aesthetic beauty of the stone, the magical properties that it was believed to possess, and the great skill that was required to carve it.

Jade is an interesting gemstone. There are actually two types of jade – jadeite and nephrite – with jadeite being the rarer and more valuable stone. Jadeite comes in several colors with the highest-quality pieces being pure green and translucent. Nephrite is a somewhat softer jade stone that is easier to carve and shape. It comes in many hues of green as well as occasionally in gray, yellow, and white.

If you are shopping for jade, **be cautioned that some of the jade you see on display has been artificially stained or dyed** to achieve a richer-looking stone and to cover up flaws. And as you evaluate a piece of jade to determine its quality and how much you want to pay for it, keep in mind that the value of jade increases with:

- **The intensity of the color**
- **The evenness of the color**
- **Its translucency**
- **Its freedom from flaws**

Jade is quite a hard stone, as measured by the Mohs scale of mineral hardness. The Mohs scale, developed in 1812 by Friedrich Mohs, ranks minerals from 0 (the softest) to 10 (the hardest). The hardness of a particular substance is determined by whether or not it can scratch another substance. So, a mineral that is lower on the scale can be scratched and marred by anything that is higher on the scale. Diamond, the hardest of the minerals, measures 10. Jade is about 7. A diamond can scratch jade, but jade cannot scratch a diamond.

Along with being hard, jade has an additional attribute that helps make it special. **It has great tenacity.** Tenacity is a gemologist's term for a material's resiliency and resistance to blows. Other gems, including diamonds, have lower tenacity than jade and can be brittle. They will sometimes break or shatter when they are hit or when they are being carved or worked on. **But jade, rather than fracturing or splitting, is a strong stone that will ring like a bell and emit a pleasant sound when struck.** This trait of tenacity allows jade to be carved quite thinly without it breaking apart so that its translucent quality can be more fully appreciated. Perhaps you have noticed this aspect of jade as you have seen jade vases, bowls, figurines, and jewelry glow as light passes through them.

Chinese grandmothers appreciate how special jade is, and although each one takes great care in selecting the proper jade bracelet, in the rare instance that a grandchild's piece of jade might break, the grandmother would actually be pleased. She wouldn't feel bad at all. She would know that some bad luck had been headed the grandchild's way and that **the jade she gave as a gift took the hit on behalf of her precious grandchild and saved it from harm.**

Although the best jade is usually found in the many fancy and upscale jewelry stores in Hong Kong, **perhaps the most enjoyable place to shop for jade is the famous Jade Market in Kowloon.** Open only during daytime hours, the Jade Market consists of two covered indoor markets featuring several hundred stalls, almost all of which sell jade. The tightly packed stalls carry numerous jade objects carved into every imaginable shape and form – rings, pendants, bangles, amulets, earrings, loose stones, figurines, bowls, and other works of art. And the prices are not set. **A fun part of shopping at the Jade Market is that bargaining is expected, so don't be shy.** If you can't get the price down to where you want it with a particular shopkeeper, move on down the aisle and try again.

Getting to the Jade Market is part of the adventure. **It is located under an overpass at Kansu Street and Battery Street.** To get there, take the MTR to the Yau Ma Tei station and take Exit C up to the street. Following the Jade Market signs, walk south on Nathan Road, turn west on Kansu Street, and you'll find the market just a short distance in front of you. (Note – There is a small Tin Hau temple near the market that you might want to explore while you are in the area.)

In the book *The Joy Luck Club* by Amy Tan, a jade pendant on a gold chain symbolizes the love and connection a mother has

with her daughter. The mother, Suyuan Woo, who is the founder of the club, knows she has just a short time to live. On page 197 of the book, we read that she passes on the precious jade pendant she has owned her entire life to her daughter, Jing-Mei Woo, **saying that it is her "life's importance."** It then becomes the daughter's turn to wear the charm and teach and inspire her own family about their heritage and the important things in life. Although Jing-Mei doesn't fully appreciate the pendant until after her mother passes away, the beautiful piece of jade becomes an important link and bond with her ancestors, mother, living family members, and descendants.

And, of course, we cannot complete our discussion of jade without hearing what the wise sage Confucius said about it. **In his book, *The Ji Li (The Book of Rites)*, he praised the eleven virtues of jade:**

The Eleven Virtues of Jade

- Its polish and brilliance represent the whole of **purity.**
- Its perfect compactness and extreme hardness represent the sureness of **intelligence.**
- Its angles, which do not cut although they seem sharp, represent **justice.**
- The pure and prolonged sound which it gives forth when one strikes it, represents **music.**
- Its color represents **loyalty.**
- Its interior flaws, always showing themselves through the transparency, call to mind **sincerity.**
- Its iridescent brightness represents **heaven.**
- Its admirable substance, born of mountain and of water, represents **earth.**
- Used alone and without ornamentation it represents **chastity.**
- The price the entire world attaches to it represents the **truth.**
- All jade is precious and dignified, for jade is **virtue.**

Jade plays a highly important role in Chinese society – including among Hong Kong's doting grandmothers. To all Chinese, the worth of jade cannot be measured by its monetary value. It is a special stone that has great symbolism and meaning and is much more precious than money. **To them, jade is invaluable.**

Chinese Term

Coolie

Coolie (gūlēi in Cantonese) is an example of a Chinese loan word that westerners turned into a bit of a derisive term. In Hong Kong and throughout China, a coolie is a strong, tough, and dedicated worker. But when thousands of them came to America and other western countries to labor on big work projects, the westerners began using the word in an offensive way, even as an ethnic slur. Coolies were often exploited, overworked, and taken advantage of by their employers.

Chinese laborers made a significant contribution to the expanding of America as they worked on projects such as the transcontinental railroad. Rather than denigrate them, we should be grateful for the coolies. **By the 1860s, almost 80% of the workers on the railroad were Chinese.** Dan Elish on pages 35 and 36 of his interesting book titled *The Transcontinental Railroad, Triumph of a Dream*, paid tribute to these laborers:

> "Many people thought it was a terrible idea to use Chinese immigrants. **After all, most Chinese were tiny, often under 5 feet tall, weighing a mere 120 pounds. How could people this small possibly be up to the physical demands of constructing a railroad over treacherous terrain?** White laborers wanted $2 a day minimum, plus board. The Chinese agreed to work for $35 a month and a small amount of money for bamboo sprouts, sweet rice crackers, salted cabbage, and other Chinese foods, which they agreed to prepare themselves. **Despite the jeers, the Chinese were impressive.** True, they couldn't dig as much dirt with a

single swing of the shovel, but they worked methodically, without talking and taking breaks. Occasionally, they would stop for a quick cup of tea, but then get right back to their job."

Although the conical-style hat worn by these workers is still sold today in stores and online as a "coolie hat," **it's probably best not to use the term anymore when referring to Chinese workers,** lest we offend them or any other of our Chinese friends.

Appendix A

Hong Kong Map

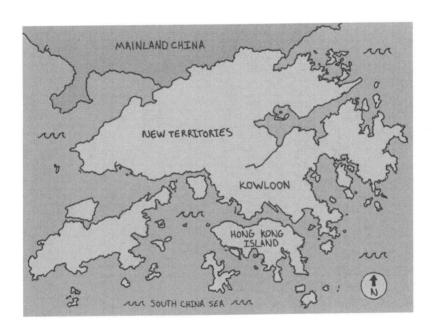

Appendix B

China Map

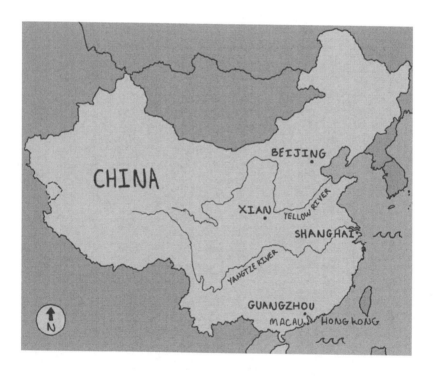

Appendix C
Hong Kong Time Line

- BC 221 – First written record in Chinese history of the Hong Kong area
- 1842 – Hong Kong Island ceded to Britain under the Treaty of Nanking
- 1860 – Kowloon acquired by the British
- 1888 – Peak Tram begins operation
- 1888 – Star Ferry begins operation
- 1898 – New Territories leased to Britain for 99 years
- 1925 – Kai Tak Airport opens
- 1928 – Peninsula Hotel opens (known as the finest hotel east of the Suez)
- 1941 – Japanese occupy Hong Kong for four years
- 1953 – Shek Kip Mei fire leads to Hong Kong's first public housing program
- 1963 – Mandarin Hotel opens (Hong Kong's tallest building at that time at 295 feet)
- 1972 – First cross-harbor tunnel opens
- 1979 – Mass Transit Railway (MTR) subway system opens
- 1996 – Lee Lai-Shan wins Hong Kong's first Olympic medal (a gold in windsurfing)
- 1997 – Hong Kong handed back to China. Hong Kong becomes Special Administrative Region (SAR) of China.
- 1998 – Chek Lap Kok Airport replaces Kai Tak Airport
- 2005 – Hong Kong Disneyland opens
- 2008 – Hong Kong hosts the equestrian events for the Beijing Olympics
- 2009 – International Commerce Centre completed (Hong Kong's tallest building at 1,588 feet)

Appendix D

101 Things to See and Do in Hong Kong

In no particular order, **here are 101 things I recommend you see and do in Hong Kong** while you are there:

1. Spend a Chinese New Year in Hong Kong. Chinese New Year spans several days and takes place in late January or early February each year.
2. Visit the Big Buddha on Lantau Island. Take the scenic Ngong Ping 360 aerial tramway to get there. After seeing Big Buddha and eating a vegetarian lunch at the Po Lin Monastery, walk to the nearby Wisdom Path. Then if you'd like to do some fairly difficult but rewarding extra hiking, go to the top of Lantau Peak, the second highest point in Hong Kong at 3,064 feet above sea level.
3. Ride the Star Ferry across the harbor at night on the upper deck. Do it again during the day on the less-expensive but more interesting lower second-class deck.
4. Have a fortune teller read your fortune using Chinese fortune sticks at the Wong Tai Sin Temple in Kowloon. Wong Tai Sin is the Taoist god of fortune.
5. Take the tram to Victoria Peak. See the beautiful panorama from the Peak Tower viewing deck. Stroll along the relaxing walk on Harlech and Lugard Roads that circles entirely around The Peak. Return to the city by tram or by walking down to the Central District via the scenic Old Peak Road.
6. Visit a Chinese cemetery.
7. See *A Symphony of Lights* at Victoria Harbour. It is the largest permanent light and sound show in the world.
8. Walk the Avenue of the Stars along the Kowloon side of the harbor where handprint plaques commemorate the icons of the Hong Kong film and entertainment industry.

9. Ride the "ding ding" (the double-decker tram) on Hong Kong Island from one end of the line to the other. Sit on the upper deck in the very front seat.

10. Watch a cricket match at the Kowloon Cricket Club. The annual Hong Kong Cricket Sixes tournament is especially enjoyable to watch.

11. Eat a Peking duck dinner at a high-class Chinese restaurant such as the Peking Garden Restaurant by the Kowloon terminus of the Star Ferry. Also, watch Peking Garden's noodle-making demonstration while there.

12. Have your name translated into Chinese and buy a chop with your name on it.

13. Ride a double-decker bus up or down Nathan Road. Sit on the top level in the very front seat. This is especially interesting to do at night when Nathan Road's multitude of neon signs are ablaze.

14. Have a suit and some shirts made for you at a Hong Kong tailor.

15. Have high tea at the Peninsula Hotel. The Peninsula is a Hong Kong landmark.

16. Buy an Octopus Card and ride the subway (the MTR) around Hong Kong. The Octopus Card is a stored-value card that can be used on the subway and other public transportation. It also is accepted for payment at 7-Elevens, McDonald's, and many other Hong Kong stores.

17. Yum cha and eat dim sum at a Chinese restaurant.

18. See the impressive 16-story silk painting of Chinese history in the Shangri-La Hotel. Titled *Great Mother of China*, it is the largest such painting in the world.

19. Watch the Hong Kong Sevens rugby tournament at the Hong Kong Stadium.

20. Go to a horse race at Happy Valley. The racing season lasts from September through June.

21. Take a cruise of Victoria Harbour on a junk. The cruise is especially beautiful at night.

22. Go to the Sky100 observation deck of the International Commerce Centre, the tallest building in Hong Kong.

23. If you have the chance, attend a traditional Chinese wedding and a traditional Chinese funeral.

24. Take a hydrofoil ferry to Macau (one hour each way) and spend the day there.

25. Attend a performance of the Hong Kong Chinese Orchestra. The entire orchestra is made up of Chinese traditional instruments and regularly presents concerts at the Cultural Centre in Kowloon.
26. Get a Hong Kong haircut and shampoo. A relaxing head massage is normally included.
27. Get up early in the morning to visit a wet market.
28. Participate in shadow boxing (taijiquan/tai chi) at a Hong Kong park early in the morning. Don't just observe. Ask the group to let you join them. They're normally happy to let you do so.
29. See the pair of giant pandas at Ocean Park.
30. Eat al fresco at one of the many restaurants at Knutsford Terrace in Kowloon.
31. Visit the Kowloon Walled City Park.
32. Attend a hearing or a trial at one of Hong Kong's higher courts of law to observe the horsehair wigs worn by many of the judges and barristers.
33. Attend the noonday gun ceremony on Hong Kong Island. This is the gun mentioned in Noel Coward's song *Mad Dogs and Englishmen*.
34. Read Mao's *Little Red Book*.
35. Purchase a bowl of steaming noodles or a cha siu pork rice box from a street vendor.
36. Go to a Chinese pharmacy and herbalist shop and ask them to tell you about the various remedies and potions offered. The proprietor, or someone else in the store, will probably be able to speak English.
37. Go to the men's room of the Felix Bar on the 28th floor of the Peninsula Hotel and observe the magnificent view of the harbor from the urinals.
38. Attend a Cantopop concert. Take ear plugs.
39. Visit one of the China product emporiums that have beautiful high-end Chinese arts and crafts. Everything in these stores is top quality.
40. Take a ferry to Lamma island and have dinner at one of the many seafood restaurants in the village of Sok Kwu Wan. Visit the floating fish and shrimp farms in the bay.
41. Watch workers erect bamboo scaffolding.
42. Shop in the crowded Mong Kok area. Visit Ladies Street, Sneaker Street, Bird Street, Shanghai Street, and Flower

Market Street. While there also visit the Mong Kok Computer Centre.

43. Ride the Mid-Level escalator from Central to the Mid-Level residential area of the island. The escalators provide a fascinating overview of Hong Kong's busy lifestyle and are the world's longest outdoor covered escalator system. Eat at one of the trendy restaurants on Elgin Street in the Lan Kwai Fong area near the top of the escalator.

44. Visit the Dr. Sun Yat-sen Museum in the Kom Tong Hall on the island. Take note of the Church of Jesus Christ of Latter-day Saints' old baptismal font on the ground floor.

45. Go to the Bun Festival that is held each May on Cheung Chau Island. This interesting island does not allow motorized vehicles.

46. As you travel around Hong Kong, look for moon gates.

47. Visit the Lei Cheng Uk tomb and museum in Kowloon. This Han Dynasty tomb is around 2,000 years old.

48. Play golf at the magnificent Mission Hills golf complex over the border in Shenzhen.

49. Buy a piece of jade jewelry at the Jade Market in Yau Ma Tei. You'll find jade there in every sculptable form. Make sure to bargain hard!

50. Visit Statue Square on the island. It is a pleasant open space amid huge buildings.

51. Attend the daily flag raising ceremony in Bauhinia Square.

52. Go to a night market, such as the Temple Street night market. Temple Street, which is closed to traffic in the evening, transforms into a very busy flea market with shops, food stalls, open air restaurants, and an occasional Chinese opera performance.

53. Take Cantonese lessons. Learn how to count from one to ten in Cantonese using correct tones.

54. Shop for golf clubs in Tsim Sha Tsui.

55. Join a group of Chinese in a game of mahjong.

56. Visit the Zoological and Botanical Gardens on the island.

57. While visiting Hong Kong, read a non-travel-type book about China or Hong Kong (such as *The Good Earth* by Pearl Buck, *Tai-Pan* by James Clavell, *The Last Governor* by Jonathan Dimbleby, or *Gweilo: Memoirs of a Hong Kong Childhood* by Martin Booth).

58. Swim in Repulse Bay on the back side of the island.

59. Drive by Jackie Chan's home in Kowloon Tong. Jackie Chan is a famous martial arts movie star who has appeared in more than 150 films.
60. Get an acupuncture treatment.
61. Play ping pong with some Chinese children.
62. Ride the #6 or #260 double-decker bus from Central to Stanley Market. Sit on the top level in the very front seat. When passing Repulse Bay, watch for the high-rise building (The Repulse Bay) on your left that has a large hole through it that was placed there in order to improve the building's feng shui.
63. Go to Hong Kong Disneyland. Ride the *It's a Small World* attraction and pay special attention to the Chinese-themed portion near the end.
64. Take lessons in Chinese calligraphy.
65. Watch a table tennis tournament at the Cornwall Street Squash and Table Tennis Centre in Kowloon.
66. Become proficient with chopsticks.
67. Observe the cooks in the kitchen of a Chinese restaurant.
68. Rent a Bruce Lee movie to watch while you are in Hong Kong. Bruce Lee was a famous Chinese action-movie star who died in 1973 at age 32.
69. Go ice skating at a rink inside one of Hong Kong's enclosed shopping malls.
70. Shop at Shanghai Tang for modern Chinese chic clothing.
71. Have the dinner buffet at the Grand Buffet Restaurant (formerly Restaurant R66) at the top of the Hopewell Center. This rotating restaurant on the island has good views in all directions.
72. Watch a lion dance and a dragon dance. They are often part of parades during Chinese festivals.
73. Watch the dragon boats during the Dragon Boat Festival in May or June. Good places to do this include Aberdeen, Sha Tin, and Stanley.
74. When served the whole steamed fish at a Chinese dinner, have the courage to eat the fish's eyeballs. They are good for you. Eat chicken feet. Try shark fin soup.
75. Visit Sai Kung and go fishing with a fisherman on a sampan. At the end of the day, take your catch to a seafood restaurant on shore and ask them to prepare it for your dinner.

76. Visit the Sam Tung Uk Museum in Tsuen Wan in the New Territories. It is an old Hakka walled village with an interesting ancestral hall and Hakka houses.
77. Go to a Hong Kong cinema and watch a Chinese movie.
78. For a genuine cultural experience, take in a Cantonese opera. Since the performances can go on for a long time, people come and go at will and don't necessarily stay for the entire opera.
79. Go to Monkey Mountain in the New Territories.
80. Early in the morning while they are hot and fresh, buy a bolo baau (pineapple bun) or a dan tat (egg custard tart) at one of the many bakeries in Hong Kong. Wash them down with some iced soya milk.
81. Eat snake soup at a snake restaurant such as the Shia Wong Hip Restaurant in Sham Shui Po.
82. Go to the performance of a Chinese acrobatic troupe.
83. Hike to the top of Lion Rock. Lion Rock is a mountain peak between Kowloon and the New Territories. The hike can be started from trailheads on either side of the mountain.
84. Visit the Ten Thousand Buddhas Monastery in Sha Tin.
85. Enjoy dinner in the evening when the lights are on at the Jumbo floating restaurant in Aberdeen Harbour. The garlic shrimp are extra good. This restaurant seats 4,000 and has appeared in many movies and TV shows.
86. Rent bicycles at Tai Mei Tuk in the New Territories and go for a scenic bike ride along the Plover Cover Reservoir dam.
87. In March during Jingzhe, watch Da Siu Yan (hitting little people) as elderly ladies seated beneath the Canal Road flyover between Causeway Bay and Wan Chai beat the photo or name of your enemy with the sole of their shoe in order to place a curse on them.
88. Eat a moon cake during the Mid-Autumn Festival in the fall.
89. Visit inside an apartment in one of Hong Kong's public housing high-rise tenement buildings. Over half of Hong Kong's population lives in public housing.
90. On a hot day, buy a mango Slurpee at one of Hong Kong's more than 950 7-Elevens.
91. Visit the Hong Kong Stock Exchange.
92. Observe the thousands of Filipina domestic helpers at the World-Wide House on Sunday afternoons.
93. Buy an antique item from one of the many antique shops on Hollywood Road.

94. Visit a government-owned public hospital (as opposed to one that is privately owned).

95. Observe the traditional pastime of men taking pet songbirds housed in beautiful bamboo birdcages for a walk in the park. (This is usually done by males, not females.) Sit in the park and watch how elderly Chinese people relax and meditate.

96. Visit the Hong Kong Museum of History in Kowloon or the Hong Kong Heritage Museum in Sha Tin.

97. Visit a classroom in a Hong Kong elementary school.

98. Watch a harbor fireworks display. Fireworks typically take place on New Year's Eve, Chinese New Year, and certain other special occasions.

99. Shop at Stanley Market on the back side of Hong Kong Island. While there, take time to visit the Murray House, a three-story building housing restaurants and boutiques that was moved stone-by-stone from Central to Stanley.

100. Go for a ride in a sampan water taxi in Aberdeen Harbour. Bargaining for a cheaper rate is expected.

101. Go to the Man Mo Temple located at the intersection of Hollywood Road and Ladder Street on the island. Note the huge coils of burning incense hanging from the ceiling of the temple. While in the area, visit fascinating Ladder Street and Cat Street to look for curios and odds and ends.

About the Author

Born in Salt Lake City, Utah, Lee H. Van Dam has also lived in The Netherlands and Hong Kong. He holds an MBA degree and is the owner of a real estate management, sales, and consulting firm.

Lee and his wife, Holly, are the parents of two children and they have seven grandchildren. They love to travel and Lee enjoys playing golf.

This is his third book. His first book is titled *Cruising – A View Through the Porthole* and his second one is *Golfing – A View Through the Golf Hole.*